To Sis Benita Evans

Write the Book

Be Blessed

Joined

Connect the right 'you' to the right people

copyright © 2014 by Robert L. Green

Scriptures noted NKJV are taken from the New King James Version.

Copyright © 1979, 1980, 1982, Thomas Nelson, Inc., Publishers

Scriptures noted NLT are taken from the New Living Translation.

Copyright ©

© 2014 Robert L. Green

Robert Green Ministries

All rights reserved. Reproduction, storage in a retrieval system or copying electronically or otherwise is forbidden without permission of the author, except for brief excerpts for purpose of book reviews.

Acknowledgment

To my Aunt, Maxine Green, I love you very much, and I pray that I will see you again someday.

To my Cousin, Latrice Maze, may you rest in peace.

To my Father, Bishop Marvin Burks, thank you for showing me the power of connecting to the right people, and being the best I can be.

To my Mother, Cluster Bailey, for the love you have shown me is priceless; I will always be indebted to you for the sacrifices you've made for me.

To my Family, for all your love and support, I thank you so much.

To my church, Redemption Ministries, your overwhelming love and support is second to none; I honor and appreciate the opportunity to serve you in ministry.

To my supporters, I want to thank you all for buying every CD, book, DVD, and other ministry product. I am grateful and I pray that these things are a blessing to your life; with your prayers and support there is much more to come.

Contents

Introduction

Part 1: Refining Me

Chapter 1   Count It Up

Chapter 2   Control - Alt - Delete

Chapter 3   Reconstruction

Chapter 4   Changing Your Mind To Change The Game

Chapter 5   The opportunity Is Now

Part 2: Restarting With You

Chapter 6   The Three Rules Of Connection

Chapter 7   Wedding Day Fine Print

Chapter 8   SEX! Give It To Me Your Way

Chapter 9   Getting Ready For Church

Chapter 10   Led To Lead

Green Note

Introduction

How do you look at the people in your life? There is a possibility that the very thing you're looking for is locked up inside somebody who is right around you. If you begin to look at the people around you in terms of the potential they display towards their purpose rather than the struggles they have gone through, it would help you understand which decisions to make and who to connect to. The power of synergy is very great; connecting with somebody that has the understanding of who they are and what they're capable of doing tips all odds in your favor. It is your God-given destiny to unlock potentials in people no matter who you are; because of *your* presence, their life should be made better.

Today's society focuses more on self-centeredness and self-gratification; if you fall into this trap you will be destined to be alone and unfulfilled, even if you're successful. One of the greatest disappointments of success is when you have made it all by yourself and nobody is around to share it with you, because selfishness will always cause your victories to be short-lived. We were never meant to be segregated, independent—this belief is a lie. That's why it's important to seize every moment by any means necessary, to make the best of every relationship that you are a part of. You fulfill this by letting go of the past; changing your mind; not remaining stagnated in the present; and setting your sights on the future. You have every means to get where you need to be.

Look around you. There is someone who has the potential and the gift to take you to the next level of your life. The Bible tells a story about a man named Joseph; he had some very difficult times because of his dreams. His dreams even got him locked up in prison where he joined with a man who was a butler and, as such, had access to Pharaoh. In this story, the butler had a dream; Joseph had the gift to interpret dreams, and by doing so, he opened up access to his destiny. Once the butler was restored to Pharaoh's service, Pharaoh had a dream that nobody could interpret; at that time, the butler remembered Joseph and his gift. This story simply reminds us that it is vitally important that we understand the power of connection. You have to view *who you are* and *what you have* as a gift, and not a personal possession. Your ability to communicate with people will ultimately propel your life into greatness, or leave you destitute and alone. Think about what would have happened to Joseph if he was only concerned about his own temporary inconvenience, and how that might have affected him from using his gift.

If you can change your mind you can change your life, and impact *everybody* that you come in contact with. The relationships in your life will be better when you change your *perspective* on the relationships and the circumstances you're in. I often say that trouble only comes to do two things: to work something *into* you, or to work something *out* of you. So be ready to fulfill your God-given purpose with a brand-new outlook on life and the people who are connected to you. It's time to bring the 'better you' to the table; maximize your life by impacting those who are in your environment.

Ephesians 4:16
New Living Translation (NLT)
He makes the whole body fit together perfectly. As each part does its own special work, it helps the other parts grow, so that the whole body is healthy and growing and full of love.

Part 1

Refining

Removing impurities or unwanted elements.

Improving (something) by making small changes, in particular making (an idea, theory, or method) more subtle and accurate.

Chapter 1

Count it up

Do you have the mental "storage" to handle a new opportunity?

Are you absolutely sure you are ready to be connected, at the right time with the right people? Connection is something that has to be thoroughly planned out. You cannot afford to take on more than you can handle, or pollute what you already have. Connecting in any sense of the word has its challenges, its pros and cons, and its ups and downs. One of the first things we'd definitely have to deal with is determining whether we have the capacity to handle the additions to our life. Whenever you're connecting with someone, you have to examine your mental capacity. You have to really ask yourself: how much *cannot* be handled? It is important to understand that you are a *limited commodity*. It is not for you to go around and try to satisfy everyone's demands and needs. Spontaneously connecting to people, places, and things can ultimately be devastating; if you have not prepared for it, it can be a breeding ground for frustration and unwanted commitment. Yet, there's nothing like receiving something you are prepared for!

I can remember one of the most exciting things that ever happened to me. Three years ago, I truly had the desire to do some remodeling at the church where I'm currently the Pastor.

This was something that was desperately needed, but I just didn't see how this project was going to happen. I knew it was badly needed, so I began to go "faith shopping". You see, this is a bit different from the typical "window shopping". Real *window shopping* is when you go and look at what you would love to have, but don't have the finances to purchase. Real *faith shopping* is when you go and locate exactly what you want; know exactly what you need; gather all the information on it; and believe that God will give you exactly what you desire.

So, I went and found exactly what I needed; it was the perfect size for the project ahead. While I stood for a long time trying out new gadgets and looking at other needed materials, I listened to the salesman give the typical "salesman pitch". As he rambled on about all the other accessories I would need to make my idea successful—punching prices into his calculator—I paused in mid-keystroke as he added up the final price. It was astronomical! I was absolutely *not* ready for the price he quoted. Eagerly, the salesman looked at me; but he could tell by the look on my face I was astounded by the number. As dollar signs flashed before my eyes, the salesman tried desperately to save the sale. He cautioned me to act quickly, because the sale on the equipment would not last long. In response, I told him I'd have to talk things over with the finance team at my church. As we walked to the front of the store he gave me his card, encouraged me to give him a call, and told me he would be more than glad to help when the finances were available. I took the card, thanked him, and assured him that I'd be back.

My head was spinning as I got into my car, because I knew in my mind that I really wanted that equipment; having it would solve so many of issues and complaints I sometimes got from some of our members on Sunday mornings. I immediately called one of the members of my finance team and explained my idea to upgrade a few things at the church. Patiently, the finance team member listened, but the final verdict was:

"Pastor, because there are a few things that are coming up for the church, we're not able to allot that amount of money to your project".

You see, the way that my mind works, I didn't hear "no"—I saw an opportunity. I replied, "what can we do? I will find a way to work this out somehow, some way."

Using her accountant's mind, she informed me how the financial plan could be completed in small increments of time. Eagerly and ambitiously I took that information, and I used that as the foundation of my masterpiece. At that moment, I was practically pulling out my hair and asking myself, *"how can I get the rest of the money?"* to finance this deal of a lifetime. All of a sudden, it hit me! To increase our church's finances, I could get rid of equipment we were no longer using, as well as some of the things that were not fully operational anymore. Once I'd sold all our previous equipment, we were halfway to where we needed to be, financially. My mind was made up, and I was determined. The other half we needed would have to come from me. At the time, I was going through some personal challenges; but I knew that, in order to get what was needed, I had to make a personal financial sacrifice for the deal to work.

A week later, I was proud to walk into the store and have the exact dollar amount to purchase what we needed. Adrenaline was pumping through my veins; I was like a kid in a candy store. I was thinking how good it would feel to walk out of the store with the equipment. I could just imagine how it would be, once we got it into the church and operating. I couldn't wait to see everybody's faces when they saw the finished product: new speakers, a newly-built booth for our sound system, and a high tech station for our camera system.

The most blissful moment was actually seeing the equipment in the church. I remember that night in March when Brother

Bowman from our church and I stayed overnight, into the early morning hours, putting everything together. We had created this space, and it looked amazing.

Sunday morning, I made sure that everything was together, so that by the time I got to church I would be able to see the expressions on everyone's faces. When the doors of the church opened, people were amazed at the drastic changes that had occurred, literally overnight. The number one question I got was, "How did you do it? We never imagined we had this much space in here to do all of this!"

I simply answered, with a smile on my face, "we took out some things we didn't need, and we made some adjustments that afforded us the opportunity to receive new equipment. I put in crazy hours to make it happen, and I had to make a personal investment to get the quality I wanted".

And all they could say was "wow, I'm glad you did! It really looks nice".

There are a lot of people you can randomly meet on the street who will tell you their dreams and aspirations; they'll also tell you the minor details that prevented them from pursuing those dreams and aspirations. Another scenario involves an even longer list of people who started projects, businesses, marriages, relationships; but due to the weight of these transitions and the commitment it would take to make it happen, they quit. They gave up! I know this is accurate, as I have been a victim of "Give Up" many times. I have gone into situations in my life with certain expectations—just like everybody else—and I honestly admit that some of my expectations were self-serving and ego-driven. Quite often, ego and selfishness can drive you into a place where you look at only the idea of the *finished product* but neglect the preparations, production, and patience that it will take to get it done. When you encourage yourself to take your purpose-filled desires [that once resulted in mere "window shopping"] and spiritually turn them into "faith shopping", you allow your faith to move mountains. Faith shopping has afforded you the opportunity to continue to make God's ministries successful for His people.

Making Space

Making space is one of the most difficult things to do, either mentally or physically. You have to literally weed out the things that are barely working and no longer useful. Go ahead and take the things that are cluttering your mind off 'life support', and make space. This is the part of the process where you realize that you can't keep *everything*—or better yet, *everybody*. I have learned that when you Let Go, God will let you Grow. When you're preparing for progress, dismissal of unnecessary things is a part of it. Things that may have worked in one area or for one season in your life may not be transferable; you need certain measurements and calculations for your new opportunities and relationships. Don't clutter your life!

Clutter is a sign of stubbornness and lack of productivity. Clutter and stubbornness almost go hand in hand. I can guarantee that the person you run into who holds a lot of clutter is not a regimented person; furthermore, that person is consistently identifying the *problem*, but never making the clear-cut decisions for *change*. This trait is very easy to detect. Have you ever been to someone's house and wanted to throw away something in the house that was outdated or broken? Or, in reality, you've actually done this and then saw an offended look on the person's face? They were offended because, in their mind, *you* have taken something personal from them that they felt was a necessity.

I daresay that one could even call clutter a spirit. There's something about clutter that can cause you to sink into a place of exhaustion, even if you are not active. You can lie down and still wake up tired and exhausted. When you find yourself in that place of exhaustion all the time, you have to take inventory of what may be draining you. The wreckage of trials and failed attempts can eventually build to clutter; Thomas Edison said:

"I did not fail 10,000 times; I just found 10,000 things that don't work".

Can you imagine: *finally* getting the one thing that works for your life—that thing that seems like it has been tailored to you from the beginning, the very thing you've been waiting for all of your life. But the joy is short-lived because you've realized that you have a mental [and sometimes, physical] scrap yard. This is a place where things that *used to* be great, and things that *used to* operate in perfect precisión are now only memorabilia of a time that is already past—a monument to an era that is long gone. In this place, you have not separated yourself from what *once* worked or pursued happiness as it exists *now*. You must have the mindset that, in order to get something *new*, you have to shed something *old.* You must put your new idea, your new business, your new relationship, or your new marriage in a place where it can stretch, grow, and blossom. Here's what the Bible says;

"Besides, who would patch old clothing with new cloth? For the new patch would shrink and rip away from the old cloth, leaving an even bigger tear than before. "And no one puts new wine into old wineskins. For the wine would burst the wineskins, and the wine and the skins would both be lost. New wine calls for new wineskins." Mark 2:22-23 NLT

Life is full of new opportunities that simply cannot be obtained with old mindsets. It is vitally important that we understand that, while there are certain things that absolutely cannot be uprooted or changed, we still have to leave ourselves open for updates. It is important that you and I update so we can have a proper analysis of where life is. This allows us the opportunity to harness the things that we need and delete the things that are no longer effective and out of season. I sincerely believe that at some point, we have to become ambidextrous to keep up with what's current, and to have a clear vision of our foundation. I ask myself time and again, *"how is it so difficult for me to let this one thing go?"* Everybody has that *one* thing that is so difficult to let go, and for some of us it can even be something that works to our detriment and ends up hurting us. In the long run, we actually foresee it happening yet we still hold on to it; but at some point each of us has to come to this conclusion: if you want something good in your life, and if you want the blessings of God to flow without restriction, you have to.......

LET IT GO!

The Apostle Paul put it so plainly when he said, *"I'm forgetting those things that are behind me".* You have to clear out old memories. You have to condition and prepare your mind for something great. You have to take the negatives and turn them into positives; so, instead of beating yourself up over past failures, take the moment to dissect what caused you to fail. Learn from the mistake, and hit the 'delete' button. There are certain things in your past that you're simply not going to be able to fix, but if you take the time to dissect what happened, you can fortify your future. Mental clutter can sometimes make you feel trapped, with a feeling of *"I don't know what to do."*

> **Green Note:** *Having a position does not guarantee promotion without test.*

Chapter 2

Ctrl – Alt – Delete

In the early 80s, IBM engineer David Bradley designed this function in Windows operating systems to solve development issues and a shortcut to start over. I think that this is a powerful principle to live by. Applying this principle in this order would revolutionize your life.

If we're going to move forward in our lives, we have to have control over our emotions and thoughts.

Before moving into right connections with other people, you've got to have this concept under control. There are certain levels of church ministry, levels of business, and levels of promotion you will never reach if your life is functioning out of control. You must come to a place in your life where you check the things that are running wild.

Promotion is the result of tests that you have passed; and nobody passes any test with their mind out-of-control. When you have centered and focused yourself on your goal, you can be promoted. You're only ready for the next level when you have discovered your personal passions. Control is a key part of every aspect of life. God doesn't use a person who is out of control; your supervisor will never use you if you're out of control, either.

So, that brings us to the point of discipline. Discipline is something that makes you stand head and shoulders above everybody else. It's one of the most powerful things that makes you attractive to those who have favor to bless you. Having the discipline to work on one specific thing continually, day after day, is a golden quality. Sometimes life can put us in a place where we are focusing on a variety of things. By not allowing ourselves the time to focus on *one* thing and not having the energy to complete the task at one time, one simple task on your 'to do' list can seem to take a lifetime.

So, what you must do is take control of your life and administer discipline. There are a lot of things that you will be 'logged out' of because of the lack of discipline. If you want to make the right connection with the right people, you can't meet them with things out of control. When this happens you look to *them* to solve the issues and bring the answers to your life; really, it is *you* who should discipline yourself and have things together so that when you meet people, you won't drag them into the tornado which is your life.

There have been many times that I've had great opportunities and, because of the chaos that was going on in my life, I was *not prepared* to use my gift at full capacity and accept the opportunity that was allotted to me. Sometimes, there had been opportunities that I'd been waiting on for months, even years. By the time I finally got to them, I was in such mental chaos—created partially by a disorderly state of mind—I wasn't able to fully utilize the opportunities. This type of blockage stops a lot of people from really maximizing their opportunities; just because you may be gifted does *not* mean you have discipline to take full advantage of opportunities presented to you.

This principle is the same across the board whether it is in the board room, the conference room, the classroom, or the sanctuary. When you're gifted, you require a greater level of discipline. This is the reason why gifted people stay frustrated: because they believe that they can do all things by using talent or their gift alone. Nothing could be further from the truth. It takes a combination of *drive* and *self-sacrifice* to get to the next level of your life. You cannot operate with things out of control. The Bible records in Joshua chapter 5 that the men had to circumcise themselves before going into the Promised Land. I believe that, before we go into great opportunities that God has given us, we have to cut away some things that are no longer needed. Controlling your life can actually be stressful, yet rewarding. You have to keep in mind that the payoff in the end is far greater than the temporary inconvenience you may be dealing with now. Bringing ourselves under control is not a one-time event, nor is it a seasonal occupation. Bringing ourselves under control will be a work that we have to continue *for the rest of our lives.*

Self-control is a part of the fruits of the spirit, which is temperance (Galatians 5:23). What it literally means is the ability to harness one's passions or lust; nothing causes more chaos and clutter in our lives than a bunch of things that we want. Satan has used every facet of media to bombard people's minds with multiple choices to entice their appetites—to the extent that they no longer abide by a moral code of conduct, but chase after the lusts of their hearts at the expense of right standards with God; a moral responsibility to family and community; and even their own betterment.

Satan has already concluded that he cannot stop you from hearing the truth; but his agenda is to overload you with so many other decisions and choices that sound true—that may be socially accepted—but ultimately bring damnation to your soul and separation from God. So, to have control in today's society, we have to have standards. We cannot be a people that are willing to try any- and everything. What we allow in our lives spiritually and physically must be governed by the word of God. God's word is all-inclusive, everything that we would ever need from A to Z is in his word. The Bible says:

A person without self-control is like a city with broken-down walls. Proverbs 25:28 NLT

A city that does not have walls is subject to any type of attack. What this tells us is the standard by which we live our lives will differentiate what comes in and out of our lives. The 'wall' that we need to have up in our minds will stop us from trying and going after lofty ideals and unrealistic expectations. It causes us to be focused on the *main* thing, and not just wondering and trying to pursue a sense of false happiness that is embedded in a carnal mind by way of sin.

A city has to have regulations and rules to abide by. Without these things there would be anarchy in whatever city you live, and this is exactly how Satan works in our lives. He wants us to mentally exist in a place where there is absolute anarchy and where you are open and accessible to anything that can destroy your soul. I believe this is why you see so many people who are extremely comfortable in the place they're currently in; but in truth, their lives are hopeless because they have allowed so many things to manifest in their spirit by way of demonic encroachment. All of Hell has organized itself against the advancement of God's people who are coming into the true knowledge and understanding of kingdom citizenship through Jesus Christ.

Yes, it's true you have the power to overcome every circumstance, trouble, and difficulty in your life by the power that already works in you, because you have received the Holy Spirit. Satan has foreseen, so he launches a plan to counteract God's truth for your life. His idea is to catch us in vulnerable places so that he can come into them suddenly. The evidence that the enemy has crept into your mind is when seeds of bitterness, hatred, and resentment become visible in your life. You try to move past certain seasons of pain in your life, but you can't seem to let those things go. Bitterness and hatred towards a person can set in, and this in turn can lead to sickness and stress—that will ultimately lead to death, all because you could not govern yourself enough to resolve issues in your life. No self-control is the seed of the enemy that has now manifested.

It is right in line with Satan's character to create recurring circumstances and situations. It may seem as though you're trapped like a hamster on a wheel; you put effort and energy into moving, but never make any progress forward. At this point, you fall into frustration and this in turn leads to compromise. Now, you find yourself trying to appease both sides—like Peter warming himself by the fire and still having his eyes on Jesus during his trial. If we don't have standards, we can find a way to have fellowship with the world *and* fellowship with Jesus. This is the type of access Satan wants; he wants to lie and take control of the wheel from you. Satan wants to drive you into a miserable existence so that you no longer view and accept God; and then, ultimately, you are turned from Him with *no control*. These things can happen.

Sometimes great people come along with the great struggles; but an even greater sacrifice is required of them.

> **Greennote:** *Set small goals first to build momentum even make a list of things that you have not completed from your past then stick to it Commit to the change.*

Alternate
Romans 12:2
New Living Translation (NLT)

Don't copy the behavior and customs of this world, but let God transform you into a new person by changing the way you think. Then you will learn God's will for you, which is good and pleasing and perfect.

One of the main things that can be poisonous to any new connection in your life is an *old mindset*. An old mindset, by my definition, was once a new mindset that hasn't yet made the proper transition into the next phase of life. There are certain things that are foundational. We cannot erase old landmarks where we have accomplished great achievements in our lives. You must become ambidextrous with your new mindset, without canceling either the old or the new. When in business, this can be very fulfilling and establish you as a credible person in whatever field that you desire to enter. Having the right credentials definitely sets you apart from those who just "wish" versus those who put in the blood, sweat, and tears to make their dreams a reality.

My thought is that you will never be successful in any area that you have not intensely studied and watched others model; but you can't get stuck there—you have to have a solid placement on your foundation and be willing to explore and investigate new ideas. Whether it is business or personal relationships, being stuck to the old ideas will bring a sense of blandness to *any* relationship, and definitely destroy the morale of any business. That's why it's vitally important to have new information—new information always sparks new ideas. Ideas cause you to navigate and alternate your directions based on the current information that you have.

I remember being about 19 years old and my father wanted me to drive him in his new car. I was thrilled and excited about the opportunity to get behind the wheel, but what I *wasn't* excited about was how he would coach me every single step of the way. On this particular day it was a little foggy, but my line of vision was clear. He warned me that there was a pothole ahead, and that I needed to get into the left lane. At the time, I remember saying to myself, *"Self, we already came this way earlier and I did not see a pothole!"*; nevertheless, out of obedience I did as he instructed and moved to my left lane. About a quarter of a mile away, I saw a construction cone that had probably been run over or kicked to the side of the road where the pothole was, *just* as he'd instructed. If I had not listened to him when he gave me the instruction, I'm sure that, as large as that pothole was, I would've caused damage to the front end of his new car.

Knowing the right time to navigate your life is priceless information that's sometimes hard to digest. This can often lead to receiving information that you'll be grateful to have later. All of us have had those moments in life and said to ourselves that it had to have been divinely inspired by God to make this right decision at the right time.

Ask yourself: *am I making the right alterations in my life? Am I adding people, places, and things that have value, or do I feel stuck with what I have, and trying to numb myself from the realities of my life?*

Are you looking at life the same way you did years ago?

Has anything changed?

It's important in this day and time to make the necessary transitional steps so that you won't overload your life with worries due to a lack of information. Without question, life can be difficult and challenging. It can also have a series of winding turns; you can't allow your mind to be emptied by outside forces over which you have no control. You must alternate your mind and soar to the level that you are called to. After pulling yourself together from tragic events of the past, you have to change your mind. Life has a lot of ups downs and some very bad paths; but ultimately those things work together for your good, to perfect the character that you need for greatness once you follow God's plan for your life.

New information causes us to think ahead. We must process the new data and make the necessary adjustments so that we can make our destination on time. There are so many people who are stuck, wounded, and hurt over things that have been said about them. People who poison others' minds may be influential people who have, at some point in their lives, mishandled, misused or abused their authority—as a result of *them* having been traumatized themselves, in certain phases of their lives. These are things that can work against you when it's time to move your mind into transitional thinking.

Making alterations can be a challenging process that's rewarding in the end. Have you ever heard the saying, *"if I could go back in time and do it all over again, I would"*? The decisions that you make today prevent you from saying this statement later. You have to seize the moment of opportunity *now*, by making some of the slightest adjustments.

It's your choice

My studies in the Bible have brought me to the conclusion that the Bible is full of *decisions*. God is the sovereign and supreme being of the universe; there is none beside Him, and there's not one like Him. Before anything could exist, He always existed. And even though He knows all these things, it pleases Him to know that we *choose* Him every day. Power and ability to have choice comes from God. We have the ability to allow things to fester or allow things to flourish. It's all up to you—you can change a large portion of every day just by simply decreeing a few things over your day before you get started. Starting and ending your day with personal devotional time with God will allow Him to give you strength and energy throughout the day, and will serve as a stress reliever at night. Choosing to make God a part of your day is one of the greatest decisions you'll ever make.

You literally have to choose to have a good day. You have to choose not to be frustrated over what's presently in front of you. You have to choose to stay the course until victory is won. It's so easy to walk away, give up, or just drop off the face of the map and completely wash your hands of a situation. But there is no victory in giving up. If you're going to obtain victory in your life, I guarantee you it will be based upon decisions that you will make. You have to look at your options and alternate your choice towards the word of God. In the book of Job chapter 23 and verse 12, Job makes the astonishing choice to put his spiritual food [which is the word of God] over his natural food, which is a necessity. To make this type of statement, you have to come to the conclusion that His word will supply your needs. If you notice yourself drifting into the same cycles over and over again, it is time to make some alterations. We were all designed by a Creator that favors success and a healthy, full life for his creation; but it is completely up to us to make the right choices.

Life has taught me that every day, I am faced with two decisions. One decision shows me my failures and my faults—and from that decision I can choose to live defeated, broken, and confused, blaming God for the Life I chose. I have so many reasons that I *could* be mean, hateful, and spiteful every day. If every time I get up in the morning I reflect on the previous day and its issues, before I know it, my bad day has turned into a bad week; my bad week turns into a bad month. But on the other side, there is my favor and my faith. I can get up in the morning and decide that, in spite of how yesterday went, I choose to have faith that God has supernaturally empowered me for this day, and this will be a good day! God has blessed me to walk in favor.

Here are some things I speak over my day:

1. **Supernatural strength to overcome**
2. **Supernatural strategy and wisdom**
3. **Prosper in every area of my life**
4. **The anointing to impact souls for the kingdom of God**

No matter who you are or what you've done, you can change your life by changing your mind.

You have to take on the mind of Christ!

Delete

Controlling yourself is difficult; making *alterations* to your faults can be very challenging; but more than anything, *deleting* people, places, and things from your life has to be done with a great deal of discretion and discernment.

It's really easy to get rid of the things that have no attachment for you; it's not difficult to get rid of something you didn't want in the first place. Like pictures on the phone that you no longer need because it takes up unnecessary space: you keep the pictures as if they're a necessity, because they're simply hard to delete. It's amazing how people make deleting look easy, but if they love a person or thing, it's actually difficult to delete. They may not show any signs on the outside, but inside they are kicking and screaming because of the pain that it takes to delete. When you get to the process of deleting what is unnecessary, you have matured to a certain level of understanding that causes you to think that there's something better in store—and what you currently have is not it. Without question, there is more in store for all of us, but we cannot be scared of the process of deleting.

If this is not your harvest, why keep it?

How long will you be afraid to move on, to give up something that you don't need for the next season of your life? That's why it is vitally important to ask God to give us this day our daily bread—the very thing that you need for today, for this season. Allow God to give it to you and let Him be your source so you won't have an attachment to something that's not Him; something that will cause you to fall into poisonous dependency. Before you connect to the right people, in the right place, at the right time, realize that you can't bring the carcass of what happened in the *past* into your *future*—you have to delete it!

Baggage

Your mindset has to be *"this is as far as this is going"—if I'm ever going to get all of the things I've heard that God has specifically and personally for me, I have to let this go.*

I'm writing this book to tell you that there is another 'you' that you've not tapped into. Understand that there is something greater on the inside of you that you have not even scratched the surface of, because of all of the things that you've had to carry in your life. There are certain life difficulties that we have to face, but living in play-by-play moments, over and over, can assassinate your joy. Just like a computer program, it is the enemy's job to keep sending you 'pop-ups' to remind you of some devastating failure that you had to experience because of poor decisions. Let's look at the story of Cain and Abel. Who do you identify with more: Cain or Abel?

Most people would think that, due to the outcome of the story, they would rather be Abel; but let's examine that view of yourself.

According to Luke chapter 11 verses 50-51, Jesus himself mentions Abel as a prophet:

He gave what was required (Genesis 4:4) (Leviticus 3:16)
He was murdered by his own brother (Genesis 4:8)
And his blood cries out to God (Genesis 4:10)

So, this story applies to you in that you were obedient to God, you gave what works were required; you had great potential; but somebody hated on you, killed your motivation, your opportunity, and your joy. Now, you're left crying out to God about what happened, as you became the victim of a tragic event.

Now, let's flip the coin and look at Cain. Cain may be considered by many to be the worst of the worst, because of his fit of rage resulting in the murder of his brother. Carefully studying this story, I began to see Cain in a different light. Reading the story over and over again, I began to wonder: I asked myself, *why didn't God Kill Cain?* According to Scripture, He had killed people for lesser offenses. There was even a man in the Bible who was struck down simply because he tried to catch the Ark of the Covenant as it fell. A caravan of people traveled with it on a cart, and the cart hit a bump in the road as the ox pulling the cart stumbled. But Cain murdered his own brother in cold blood; God had all the evidence against Cain, and yet he allowed him to live.

Here's my perspective on the story: God gives unconditional love and overwhelming mercy. If you notice at the end of Genesis chapter 4, Cain has a wife and he builds a city then has children and even grandchildren with the name of God embedded in their names. The key point of the story is this: despite what you have done in the past, if you have breath in your body you have the opportunity to move on and still do something great in spite of whatever you messed up. You can't live in a place of defeat. Forgive yourself and move on, you still have greatness inside of you. Don't allow yourself to be hung up over shortcomings—'delete', and get ready for something great.

Psalm 106:28
New King James Version (NKJV)
They joined themselves also to Baal of Peor, and ate sacrifices made to the dead.

Living in the Cemetery

Are you holding grudges for long periods of time? Even though people have come to you to try to resolve the issue and move on? Time has gone by, but you drag the memories of that particular event with you. In the mounting silent rage, your emotions are clearly seen in your actions from those prior incidents, because you have not been healed from the memory. Even though the situation is long past for you, the emotions are still very real and relevant. Now, you're beginning to replay the memories of those incidents in your mind whenever you have to see the person with whom you hold a grudge. The fact is that when you see them doing well and going forward in life, it restarts the movie entitled *"How You Hurt Me"* in your mind all over again. You think about moving ahead; but honestly, if you could take the revenge that you wanted, it *still* would not stop the recurring thoughts you have about that hurtful place in your life.

Take my advice: go ahead and bury *every* dead situation in your life. There's no need to nurse dead situations hoping to get your life back out of it. Go ahead and let it die, if you're going to be connected to the things designed by God that are going to better your life. The only way that will happen is if you let go of past situations. Ashes to ashes and dust to dust; the more you harbor it, the more it will hinder you. If you don't release these things, they will spill out of your past into your attitude towards a new connection. Holding on to pain and discouragement will eventually contaminate you, or even dissolve something great in its beginning stages—something that has been introduced into your life to bless you.

You can't be a hoarder of hurt feelings and disappointment; you have so much more to live for than to carry around old junk. Can you imagine what it must be like for people in your life to come into your personal space only to be hit by the stench of dead relationships hidden in the closet of your mind? *Clean out your closet!* Make a conscious decision to create room for something better. Don't hinder your life by holding onto something useless—get rid of it, don't let it assassinate passion and kill your drive. The longer you hold on to stuff, you'll find yourself *breathing* but not *living*. Let it go.

> **Green Note:** *The weight of guilt and shame could be a reason why people have not rectified their wrongs with you. Don't allow this to hinder you. Forgive anyway. Let it go, and live life.*

Chapter 3
The Reconstruction of Me

Joshua 5:8-9 NKJV
So it was, when they had finished circumcising all the people, that they stayed in their places in the camp till they were healed. Then the Lord said to Joshua, "This day I have rolled away the reproach of Egypt from you." Therefore the name of the place is called Gilgal to this day.

Stay in your place

After going through the process of cleaning out what you don't need; bringing yourself under control by alternating your thoughts; and leaving behind the painful memories of bad decisions, *don't move too quickly*! One of the grave dangers of coming out of a bad situation is jumping right back into another one without taking the proper time to heal from what you've been through. You need time to process what has happened to you, then address the issues before successfully moving on. I have learned that, in a season of healing, two things normally happen:

1. What normally happens is you find yourself alone. People who have watched you from afar that *wanted* to reach out and help you did not, because of your decisions. In most cases these are the people you overlook; these are the ones who have wisdom and knowledge—they have been around you all the time but, because of the mental tornado that you have been in,

they've become almost invisible to you. A lot of times, these people that you underestimate and believe will never understand what you are going through actually know *exactly* what you have been through; they know exactly what it's like to be in your shoes. They are loaded with great testimonies that would change your life if you ever took the time to open up and receive what they're saying.

2. A lot of times, God allows a healing process; you have previously depended on so many people that He allows you to find yourself in isolation so He can perfect and build in you *what you need for the next level of your life.* In this process of isolation, He heals you from the circumstances and issues that have remained beneath the surface. Remember that God has the ability to search the deep things that are hidden in our hearts. When you're in the season of healing and God has you in isolation, dragging another person into it is like prison to them. You have to know when to welcome people into your space, and you have to know when it's a season that you need to be alone and seek God. Let Him give you peace of mind.

In dating people, we often exchange stories about the dramatic, emotional war stories that we've been through in life; but very rarely do we ever say what we have been healed from. It's important to know that the person that you will date, or befriend, or enter into business with has closure on old situations. If they don't, leave them alone until they do. It's best to allow people the proper time to heal. We can be 'antsy' and anxious to jump into something new, but if you would just take a little time to completely shed the old 'you' with the old mindset, you would bring a better 'you' with a better mindset to the table. And that's why if God has you in a healing process for a particular season, *it is best to stay in your place.*

The Season of Preparation

The next season that God brings you into is a season of preparation. In this season, you begin to prepare for what you have planned. This is the season where you stretch out on your faith and get your hopes up again. In this particular season, the enemy often pulls out all the stops to make sure that you are distracted from what's ahead. You're at a place of maturity now where you have shed the old things and the old mindset. In the season of preparation, you must allow the Holy Spirit to come into your life and take residence so that a metamorphosis can take place in your life. Don't allow guilt to stop you in your tracks; you have to believe and tell yourself, *"I am healed, no matter what the enemy shows me."*

Stay focused. Satan is an expert 'counterfeit future' salesman when it comes down to phony offers. The enemy would love to throw you into a busy intersection of decisions so that you won't be able to focus and you'll end up re-creating predicaments you have already avoided. His mindset is if he can't *destroy* you, he'll *distract* you; but you have come too far for that.

Getting Ready for Something Great

Driving home one Sunday evening from church, I received a phone call from a guy by the name of John who used to be a neighbor of mine. On my arrival in Iowa years ago, he was one of the first people to come and actually hold a conversation with me and make me feel welcome to the neighborhood. Even though we had our different beliefs when it came to how we worshipped, what we did not dispute was who we worshipped. We would consistently go back and forth about certain issues and topics that were very important to us. Looking at the caller ID, I was still in amazement as I said "hello". We took a few moments to catch up, and he asked me to come over to his house. He told me that he'd really gone through some difficult struggles, and he just needed somebody to pray with him.

"I'm sure after all the singing, shouting, and dancing you should be tired, but I really need you to come over to my house," he said.

I replied, "Whatever! I'll be over there in about 15 minutes. You called me while I was on the other side of town, but I'll be there shortly."

As I arrived at John's apartment complex I thought to myself, *he must have downsized, because this area and this place is not him at all.* I went into the apartment building looking for apartment #205, and I finally found it at the end of the hall. I knocked on the door and heard his voice say, "just a minute." I waited a few seconds as he opened up the door.

I asked John, "how's it going?." and shook his hand.

"It is good, Rev!," he answered, "come on in."

as I walked in I saw that John had downsized from a three-bedroom to an efficiency. I walked in and looked around to see that John had everything neatly stacked and organized, just like it was when he was in the three-bedroom; John was clean as a whistle. He offered me something to drink, which I declined, then I walked over, sat down on his bed, and took off my jacket.

He said, "wait a minute! You're welcome to the chair, but don't sit on my bed."

I replied, "Dude! Why are you acting like that? All you've got is a hard wood chair; man, you can sit in that but I'm sitting on the bed, it's more comfortable for me stop—treating me like you don't know me."

John's reply to me was that the chair was for guests and the bed was for the host. He let me know that although things had changed, the same rules applied in the *efficiency* just like they had when he was in the three-bedroom.

He told me, "Look, don't be mad at me because I'm a man of structure and order."

I said to John, "yeah, you're right"—but I still thought he should let the guests sit comfortably and be a gracious host; I got up, and after that we began joking about something we'd both seen on the news. We talked about another two hours about things that were going on in his life; I prayed with him, and I left.

As I was driving home, the incident replayed in my mind and I began to have a deeper understanding for what he was saying. I believe we'd both just acted out a critical principle that stops the growth of ministries.

Let's put this story in the terms of the church. The church has been commissioned by God in the Holy Scriptures to invite people of all walks of life to be a part of the kingdom of God, but there is a great deficiency when you have members of any organization that have the mentality of efficiency. This pathology causes people to come into an organization and become resistant to structure and order that propels them to grow; so psychologically, they gravitate to things that are familiar because it takes less effort—anything that calls and challenges them to grow is too much.

Busy Intersections

The hustle and bustle of everyday life sometimes weighs us down to the point that we make hasty and rash decisions based on temporary inconveniences.

One thing's for sure about life: it is full of decisions; the more life you have, the more decisions you have to live with. If you are like me, you spend a lot of your life thinking, *I should have taken another route, man!*

At the age of 34, I look back on my 20s and say to myself, *"if I could just get 10 years back, I would have done 1,000 things differently."*

I cringe when I look back over my life and look at all of the time I've wasted on things that were irrelevant. There's something about maturity that links the shock factor when you look back over what you could've done. I'm not the one to cry over spilled milk, but sometimes you have to take inventory over your life to make sure of things.

Life can be a busy intersection, with things coming and going to the degree that it's difficult to find a foundation to build on. Have you ever been introduced to something really quickly, and the way it was presented it seemed to be a sure thing; but after some time and observation, you saw that you'd made a terrible and sometimes binding mistake? Then, you think to yourself, *had I just taken time to think the matter over, I would've made a totally different decision.*

Timing

Timing is a key element when you find yourself at the crossroad of your life. It seems like things are going so fast, but you've got to remember timing.

I believe that, to be great in anything, you have to have timing. Just because you're skilled or anointed to do whatever it is you do, does *not* guarantee a high level of effectiveness in any season. For example, as an up-and-coming artist in the music industry, no matter how hot the album is the new artist still has to be conscious of major, established artists. Any artist would tell you they want their project to drop at the *right time,* when the industry needs the style of music they deliver.

Collisions in life happen when you don't take the time to strategize your movement. Movement without direction can bring about frustration. You have to honestly know where you're going, what you're doing, and most importantly, *why* you're doing it.

With so many things pulling on us in life, we have to have clear direction. With your potential and the path that you're following, this is one of the greatest reasons why it is so difficult to center your mind. The negative forces, or—better yet, Satan—has a calculated plan of attack against your mind because he knows if he can contaminate you, he can also detain you. Clear-thinking people who are not entangled in unproductive thoughts are the enemy's worst nightmare. That's why Psalms 27:11 says:

Teach me thy way, O LORD, and lead me in a plain path, because of mine enemies.

So, in order *not* to get caught in the intersection of real life and be unprepared to make great decisions, you must decide to consult God on the correct timing for everything you do. People often say that they consult God before making decisions; but in reality, what they do is pray but *don't wait for an answer.* Then when it seems as if the answer is taking too long, we will privately consult our own options and concoct a *self-made* answer to the question that we've asked God. In reality, we should have taken the time to count up the costs, as the Bible says, so that we will not become impatient and make a wrong turn down a street we don't want to be on.

Life can move so fast, it seems like it forces you to make quick decisions; but I guarantee you, the decision that is well thought-out is the decision that you'll be confident of and will feel good about. Nobody *accidentally* went from poverty to prosperity; in some cases, they've worked and prepared for very long periods of time for the one moment that would change their lives. Sometimes, what's quick is cheap.

If you ever want any level of durability in your life, there is a certain price that has to be paid; if you plan to expand your capacity in any facet of life, there is a certain price that absolutely must be paid with no negotiations.

From a biblical perspective I honestly don't see randomness, but I see strategy with studying the Bible; I see the integration of the Scripture having multiple writers on different continents over the span of about 2,000 years. The message is still planned and deliberate. The Bible gives this away when it says the book was written of me (Psalms 40:7)

The old saying is right: hindsight is 20/20. To be perfectly clear, I think I've I spent a lot of my life in fear of what would happen if I moved in a certain direction; how would I be accepted? I have oftentimes thought that it's fear that will cripple faith if you allow it to take over. God gives clear-cut directions, but can be vague on the conditions of where you're going. Jesus will tell you 'get in the boat, let's go to the other side'; but He won't mention the storm that's going to take place in the transitional period of moving to the other side. Why? Because He is the Creator of the universe, everything works according to the counsel of His will. There's absolutely nothing that can happen that He is not aware of, and He is sure and confident in the gift and ability that He is giving you. So we must trust Him with our faith and anticipation for what is getting ready to transpire in our lives. Have faith in the supernatural ability that God has invested in your life by way of the Holy Spirit. The Holy Spirit is the absolute only way that we can receive the great things that God has prepared for us.

Balancing Your Watch

Procrastination is no longer an option. We have to be more time-sensitive and time-conscious of everything we do. Procrastination often comes from devaluing the significance a person holds for a place or thing. You have to have the proper balance of movement; you can't move too fast or think that you can't procrastinate, either. You have to plan strategically to move at the appropriate time, and that is only given by divine inspiration from God. In a new place in your life, there are always things that you didn't think were that important that you miss when they're gone; so many times we say *"if I could go back in time"*, but the thing about making this statement is that you'll never be able to go back in time—you can only maximize the opportunities in the moments here and now. You have no time to waste in pointless and meaningless conversations and situations. For the next level of your life, you can't afford to go in distracted; how you start is very important. You can't stand by idly and wait for perfect sunny days to do something. You have to move *when it's time to move*. There'll be times when God tells you to move when there's perfect sunshine, the birds are singing, the wind is blowing through your hair, and it's a perfect day where you will actually *feel* like moving. And on the other hand, God may tell you to launch out into the middle of a thunderstorm; when everybody else is running for cover may be when He tells *you* to step out.

Now that the healing process is over and preparation has already taken place, this is the time for you to make a move. Arm yourselves with the things that you have learned from your past mistakes in previous times. You have to take this opportunity in life to do more to build your faith; if you're not building your faith, you're feeding your fear. Shed yourself of your fear and stop letting disappointments cripple you. All of us have been disappointed; if you're going to go forward in your life and into the good success that God has promised you, there's going to be some disappointments—but if you're wise, they will be minimum.

One of the greatest teachers we'll ever have in life is experience. So, if that is the case, the *worse* off your life has previously been, the *better* armed and dangerous you will be as you're going into your destiny. When you're preparing for something great, I dare say that you even need to examine the way you dress, because you will be compared on the inside as well as the out. There's a saying that states, "you don't get a second chance on first impressions". I absolutely believe that. Of course, your dress isn't more important than your character; but wherever you're trying to go, you should look like you *belong,* and that your character qualifies you to be there.

> **Green Note**: *Desperation causes you to choose unclear avenues. The fear of lost opportunities results in quick and myopic decisions that bring you to temporary solutions you will ultimately pay for at the wrong time.*

Chapter 4

Changing your mind to change the game

> **Green Note:**
>
> *"Applied understanding = growth."*

Distortion & Distinction

Clarity is one of the most important things in the world of communication. By this, you can determine the amount of time applied to the relationship. The number one enemy of relationships of any kind is distortion.

The word distort means: *to twist out of a natural, normal, or original shape or condition.*

How many times have we been in situations that called us to be in a distorted delusion because we did not check the facts? I hate that, in some relationships, we sell people on the idea of our *dream* and not *reality*. This has great potential for danger, almost as if you were to open your front door of your home, walk in, and smell smoke. The only difference between an actual fire and a distortion is that you can't smell the smoke. When you first meet someone, it is very important to take note of where they have been, their goals, and how long they've been trying to achieve their goals. Spend time listening to their *dream*, but study their *drive*.

Drive is the determining factor to every dream. Drive is the most important thing when it comes to fulfilling your purpose. A healthy dose of drive is like medicine, and just like medicine, too much can be harmful to healthy connections; high doses of drive can turn into ambition. Ambition then leads you to distortion to fulfill your drive.

It's not wise to connect yourself to somebody that's overly ambitious, because—not initially, but eventually—you will be viewed as a stumbling block or a hurdle to get over when you try to bring things back into reality. In most cases, you go from being comrades to competitors. You can never achieve success with a comrade who has made you an opponent. Most of the time, they look at you as an obstacle or a game they must win. If it were a race, they wouldn't care anything about coming in 10th place, as long as you came in 11th. They said their goal was to win the race, but their drive was to beat you. Please, don't get me wrong—a certain amount of competitiveness is helpful to keep each other conscious of our aspirations and dreams, and it keeps us from being stagnated. When distorted manipulation tricks are used to win an object or goal, this is harmful to relationships or business associates. There is absolutely no manipulation like using the *truth*, but bending all of the *facts*. This allows the manipulator to say 'I was telling the truth"—they just leave out all the important, necessary facts. Have you ever visited certain websites that advertise Free! Free! Free!—until you get ready to purchase. Or better yet, they advertise that everything is absolutely free, *except* for the shipping and handling costs—and then they remind you of all the other free products they have. See, the object here is to keep your mind on the word 'free'. As long as your mind is on the word "free", subconsciously you feel better about the shipping and handling costs. Do you see where I'm going now? *Overly ambitious people use distorted truths to keep your mind on dreams and not on all the things that you have to lose in order to accomplish it.* It's best to just go ahead and tell the truth up front, so everyone that may be joined into any agreement will have a clear-cut understanding about what it takes for a goal or dream to be reached.

Distorted truths are like preparing a recipe where almost all your ingredients are good, but you have one whose freshness date is expired. You don't really have to use the expired ingredient, but out of desperation or manipulation you use it anyway—and you serve others this dish with its tart taste, hoping that nobody will notice it. These things do damage to everybody that is involved; that's why it's best to go ahead and tell the truth, and get it all out-of-the-way rather than to keep trying to bandage something that needs to be cleansed and stitched and healed over time.

> **Green Note:** *" it would be best to be broke by the truth, than to be rich with lies"*

Identifying Distinction

For the next season in your life, one of the main components for success will be wisdom. Wisdom gives you the ability to discern between different things that may look similar. This is one of the most neglected issues in today's culture, because this discernment is something that cannot be "microwaved" or birthed overnight. It takes great patience and submission to someone who has wisdom that you don't have. Nobody will ever be able to say "I didn't learn from anybody". The Bible plainly tells us that there is nothing new under the sun—somebody has already gone before you and done it before you, so it would be best to learn from a mentor who has wisdom.

There is a vast difference between being *smart* and being *wise*. The two are not the same at all, in any facet of life. Reading books can make you smart; but submitting to a leader, becoming a servant, and studying *along with* reading books will make you wise. If you're going to make the *right* decisions, and find the *right* person or thing for the *right* job, you need the ability to discern which ones are *not* right, and that only comes about by wisdom.

One of the greatest things we can ever do in life is to discover our difference, just like Joseph, Esther, Ruth, and Daniel. The Bible shows us that all of them were promoted because somebody with higher authority saw a distinct difference in them.

Your willingness to be used to solve problems makes you stand out in a crowd. Think about it: nobody wants a liability in their life or business, you seek out somebody who can solve problems. Some people encounter problems and they mentally unravel; but when you have wisdom in approaching a problem, you become energized because you know that you can find a solution. Wisdom is very important; I believe it's so important, you'll need much more wisdom than you will ever need money. There are certain things that money cannot buy, but wisdom can. The Bible says:

Proverbs 4:7-8   New Living Translation
Getting wisdom is the wisest thing you can do!
And whatever else you do, develop good judgment. If you prize wisdom, she will make you great. Embrace her, and she will honor you.

Money can sometimes be viewed as a necessity, but the impact of wisdom is far greater and goes far beyond money. When you develop in wisdom, it's highly probable that you will make the right decisions. Wisdom is a necessary key for success, that's why in this season it is absolutely important that you pray for the wisdom of God. You cannot do it on your own, and you must change your perspective from inward to upward. It will be the greatest decision you ever make in life.

When God gives us wisdom and divine direction, we cannot allow our carnal mind to get in the way. It is our human nature to try to find a rational way to explain things and do things on our own. There is a natural instinct—just like Adam and Eve in the garden—to cover ourselves, because we are not used to being open and getting in front of anybody, including God; but I'll deal with that later on.

Self-dependency is often born of the environment that we've had to adapt to while growing into maturity. Yes, sometimes it can be difficult to let go of the wheel, but I guarantee that if you let go, *God is a better driver.*

Don't depend on yourself

I have arrived at this conclusion, having looked back over my life at the horrible decisions and mistakes I've made out of immaturity and a selfish will. There are so many things that God wanted to bless me with, but out of stubbornness I just couldn't see it. Stubbornness will always be an enemy of change; stubbornness will always keep us cold, bottled up, and alienated. Have you ever wanted to kick yourself for the opportunities you missed because you were stubborn? For me, the majority of those opportunities required me to depend on somebody else. When you're accustomed to doing things alone, then find that you must work with someone whose trust is required in order to finish a task, it's difficult to let go of complete control. You're so used to depending on yourself that at someone else's slightest error, you forfeit the agreement and isolate yourself out of fear of disappointment—when, really, all that's needed is more communication and recalibration. A lot of times, trust issues result from expectations that are set higher for *others* than you would set for *yourself*; and the minute someone does not meet your expectations, the connections you have with them are on the chopping block.

In times past, I have been in isolation myself because people have disappointed me, so I proceeded with the "I'll just do it myself" attitude, rather than to deal with people. In reality, you cannot go through life without dealing with anybody else. In dealing with others there will be a certain amount of problems, dysfunctions, and errors—and that is absolutely inevitable. You can't go through life like a jar with the lid on so tight that nobody can open it. In most cases, the way we treat God reflects same way we treat other people—and we really won't open up to Him, either.

Regretfully, there are many people who are caught up in that "I can do it myself, I don't need any help from anybody" syndrome. I often acted as thought I was on an isolated island out in the middle of nowhere, where nobody could find it or go there. It's as though it's reserved for only you, and on this island you have no contact with anybody else.

Have you ever heard the statement *"you have to believe in yourself"*? Although this statement is true, it's key to know that, in order to have relationship, family and community, we also need to believe in each other. The enemy specializes in making you feel displaced and all alone. I believe that this is a Satanic agenda against believers and against God's *first, original* institution which was family, and then, community. I believe that Satan's plan has been the same since Genesis chapter 3; it basically has not changed, but his methods may have alternated throughout time—that is still the same. The strategy for tempting Eve was convincing her, *"you are missing something, and the only way you'll get it is if you do it yourself"*: disobeying God and taking matters into her own hands. Think about it: the reason why she even took the fruit was because of the pursuit of being more like God, and to be wise, which is also written in John's first epistle as he echoed Genesis 3

1 John 2:16 (NKJV)

For all that is in the world—the lust of the flesh, the lust of the eyes, and the pride of life—is not of the Father but is of the world.

If we're going to embrace the fact that we are Kingdom citizens, as the Bible plainly states, then it is absolute treason to have a will other than the King's. Satan is very proficient at being a deceiver. He knows that it would be beyond difficult to get believers to worship and be devoted to him, so his present disguise is self-promotion. By very simple but effective methods, many of us have been led astray.

1. Break up unity through distrust.
2. Isolate you, and flood you with mixed emotions.
3. Bring you back together amongst others, and show you how you don't fit in.

4. Give the illusion that the only way to stop the mental agony is to turn from God's principles and laws by finding your own way.
5. Convince you that you are alone and have no one; you must depend on yourself.
6. Convince you that you can be independent and make it—look at all the others who do; maybe the way of Christ just isn't for you.

Satan's tricks are easily seen. Even though he is trying to manipulate you, God's word still stands for sure—you have to trust in it and believe it. So, before you go after the pursuit of happiness and security for your life, please know that all of those things have already been factored into God's master plan.

Proverbs 3:5-6 (NLT)
Trust in the Lord with all your heart; do not depend on your own understanding.
<u>Seek his will in all you do</u>, *and he will show you which path to take.*

We have to live life totally dependent upon Him. We cannot fall to Satan's plan of self-promotion, because it only gets us demoted by God. We can't go counter to His will. He already wrote the will for our lives; we must fully trust and believe in

Him in order to see His plan clearly. We have to depend on Him because He is greater than we are, the Bible declares:

Isaiah 55:8-9 (NLT)
"My thoughts are nothing like your thoughts," says the Lord. "And my ways are far beyond anything you could imagine. For just as the heavens are higher than the earth, so my ways are higher than your ways and my thoughts higher than your thoughts.

Psalm 61:2 (NLT)
From the ends of the earth, I cry to you for help when my heart is overwhelmed. Lead me to the towering rock of safety.

We all have to realize that we were not just left here on Earth like an experiment gone wrong that's left on the shelf. God has not aborted his plans for us. He is fully confident of His saving power; the issue is getting his 'crown jewel'—which is human kind—to trust Him without waver or doubt. Circumstances and situations will always tempt us to change God's priority status in our lives; but this is the most detrimental thing that we often do. We have to break the cycle of thinking independently and start thinking of *self* and *God* as a corporation. When it comes down to direction and what's best for the company, major decisions have to be brought to the table and discussed with the person in charge in order for us to have the success that we need in business. You absolutely have to trust that the direction you're going in is orchestrated and filtered by God.

Don't allow the old mind to try to reposition itself in the driver's seat, because you can't afford to be stuck in the same position year after year, time after time, season after season. This time, do not only *make a change,* but *commit to the process* that change brings—don't go back into the former way of thinking. To say that you trust God means more than you just believing that He exists. You also have to believe that He is the sovereign authority over all things, and that all things work according to the counsel of His will. So, before this book begins to talk about connecting with *people*, the number one priority is to make sure, fully sure that you're connected with *God* first. Putting God's principles first allows you to look at things from a different perspective and causes you to utilize principles that the average person may not understand or agree with. But using God's principles that are in his Holy word is almost like having the inside scoop on something before it hits the public. That's why believing Jesus Christ and receiving the Holy Spirit is so urgent before you connect with anybody. In doing this, it positions you in the right place; and when you're positioned in the right place, your mind is clear and you have the ability to focus on what is important, long-term as well as short-term. When you're connecting with anybody at any level of your life, it is important to have spiritual discernment that comes by way of the Holy Spirit.

My personal experience with the Holy Spirit has allowed me to see things in a completely different light. It has allowed me to see things for what they really are. There were moments when I was getting ready to make life-altering decisions, but the Holy Spirit intervened and turned the situation around and altered my decision for my good. If you do not have the Holy Spirit I encourage you, my brothers and sisters, to honestly allow Him to come in and live within your heart and your mind.

Battery Operated vs. Power Outlet

Early one morning I got a call to ride out of town for a brief turnaround trip with my friend, Dawson. I had some free time on my schedule, so I decided to go along with him just to have a change of scenery. As we were riding, we were talking about some of our ideas for our churches. A period of silence went by, and then he asked me, *"what's the difference between batteries and a power outlet?"* My response to him was that one is made for portable use, and the other is made for stationary use.

"You're right, but let's cut a little deeper," Dawson said.

So many people are caught up in 'flexibility', the ability to go wherever, whenever you want to and not be tied or connected to anything or anybody. And because they do not want to stay in one place long enough, they will settle for an insufficient power source that will cause them to have to live in inadequacy, looking for somebody to replenish what they've lost. The more they do, the less energy they have. On the other hand, being connected to a power source does not give you the accessibility to go as you please and do whatever you want to; however, the pros significantly outweigh the cons at all times. As long as you're connected, you can do and fulfill the purpose for which you were created. It may not be glitz and glamour and gold, but consistency, reliability, and faithfulness are attributes that are priceless and rarely found in our society today.

Metaphorically, this story applies to so many people who would give up consistency and reliability for flexibility, with no contract. The more that we fall into this trap, we find ourselves exasperated by the decisions we've made to try to compensate for the things and the energy we've spent in the wrong places.

It's important that we understand the lesson of staying connected to God. There's so much stress in life that comes from our straying away from God's principles.

Storm Chasers

This is a dangerous job, because of the potential damage that can happen to the individual just by the winds alone, not to mention the debris. These brave individuals risk their lives to get as close as they possibly can to a storm, closer than anyone else has before; the more dangerous and violent the storms are, the more enthused they are about going after it.

Here's a lesson we can learn from reality TV: if you see yourself walking into a dangerous situation, you can't have the idea you're going to change a person's will. When you try this, there's a great possibility you will not get the authentic 'them', but an off-brand version of them, because they can only keep up the façade for so long. Here's what will happen: things will be going well when they meet you on your turf, but the minute that you try to get close to them, you'll be hit by the debris from their past or present life. Because they refused to resolve their issues, they just keep moving from place to place. You normally see this type of behavior in a person who has had a lot of good opportunities afforded to them, but for some reason there's always an underlying issue—it's *someone else's* fault that they are not in their position or relationship anymore. The truth of the matter is, you can't save anybody until they're willing to break this cycle. Until then, you'll be dodging the debris and weathering the storm until they're ready to stop and deal with the decisions they've made that brought on this disaster.

Part 2

Restarting with You

Chapter 5
The opportunity is now

Take Advantage Of Now

Every moment in life is precious. Every opportunity, every connection that you will make will benefit and profit you. It will either profit you by allowing you to gain more to continue for better living; or it will give you a stress test to see if you have really committed to the changes you have made in your life for the good. You must understand that you make history *every time you step foot out of the bed*. When you get up in the morning, you can set your data to make great memories or lousy excuses. Studying some of the people who are successful, rich, and at the top of their game, all have one thing in common: they have a multitude of failures behind them. They have tons of critics throughout the process, but none of that stops them. Why? You have to believe in the purpose that you were created for and hold onto it, because the life that God has called you to live actually *does* depend on it.

So seize the moment, seize every opportunity for advancement that the Holy Spirit reveals to you. Don't waste any more time wondering whether or not <u>this</u> is the moment and the opportunity for your life; in order for you to go forward, you have to believe that God has already blessed you and granted it to you.

Don't become the mayor of "IF Ville"

Seizing opportunities requires a bulletproof mentality that cannot be penetrated by the "**What If's**" in life. Worrying about the outcome of every situation can sabotage you before you even get started. The truth of the matter is, it's not just the good things that make us who we are but it's also the bad things and bad mistakes that we have made in the past. The lack of faith and hope will cause high levels of anxiety to invade your mind. Because of past experiences, you can begin to prejudge and underestimate the opportunities and people that are all around you. Turn your "what if" in to "I Can"—don't under estimate yourself, go for it.

The Dutch discovered Australia 100 year before the British, but thought it was worthless and ignored it.

Russia sold Alaska to the US for 2 cents an acre because they thought it was worthless.

What opportunities have you underestimated because of your mind set?

Years ago I worked at a uniform warehouse, and I only worked there for the pay; it was boring until they hired Aaron. He was the type of person who could win anybody over to his cause. I had the responsibility of training him, but looking back now, he was actually training *me*. He would always take the bus to work. To make sure he was early, he always got to work way ahead of time so he could set up his station before the shift started. Me? I got there just in time to not be late, and sometimes I did not make it.

Aaron would always joke with me and say "Green, you're the veteran, how am I ahead of you?"
My response to him was, "man! I'm just trying to get paid, that's all I really care about. You can do all of that if you want to, but I'm just trying to get a check, and I'm out of here."

"Man, I hear you," he replied, "I'm trying to get paid too, but I'm trying to get promoted to go up front in the office," he said. "It's pointless to keep coming here and doing the same thing over and over again—to keep unloading trucks. Wait-and-see, after a while—a couple of more months—they will be asking me to come up front; you watch and see."

"Man, you're crazy," I told him. You're not going up front, all they want us to do is unload trucks—that's it."

"That's what *you* think," Aaron said, "there's no way possible that I am going to continue to stay in the same place."
I felt that I was way more qualified and had far more skills than I was using to unload trucks. Most of the jobs that I'd had could potentially advance to the management level; I may have

made some stupid decisions in the past, but that had nothing to do with my qualifications.

10 days later, Mr. Jamison, the CEO of the company decided to pay our branch a visit. Coming out of the front office walking side-by-side with our supervisor, Tony, the CEO immediately noticed Aaron. As he got ready to cross Aaron's path, Aaron immediately stopped what he was doing, walked towards the man, and reached out his hand.

"Welcome, thanks for the opportunity to work for you," Aaron said, "it's been a pleasure. Tony has made me feel welcome and a part of the family these last couple of months".

"Glad to meet you, young man. You have a lot of spark," Mr. Jamison told Aaron. "That's the kind of enthusiasm we need in this company."

"Yes, he is one of our rising stars," Tony said.

After overhearing this conversation, I began to feel jealous and said to myself, *why didn't he say anything about me? I'm more qualified...I hate this job!*
Aaron walked back to his station and began working again.

"You happy now, 'company man'?" I asked him.

"You're just mad that I'm getting ready to go up front to work in the office," Aaron said.

"Yeah yeah," I said. "Well, company man, we've got another truck coming in 20 minutes."

What I learned from this particular story in my life was how I procrastinated on things I should have been way ahead of. What Aaron taught me is that you have to seize every opportunity, no matter what it is. The Bible teaches that you can't despise small beginnings; nobody starts right at the top, and just because you put in a little bit of time does *not* make you qualified—it's how you apply yourself with the time you have.

Once I got the revelation, from that point forward I began to look at opportunities differently. I found that the more I would procrastinate, the more I wanted other people who were trying to seize their opportunity to *slow down*. Have you ever heard people say, "it does not take all of that"?. A lot of times, this is what you hear from people who consistently procrastinate; they have no idea nor can they understand why you applied that much energy, because they feel nothing is going to happen. Their expectation has been tainted with frustration, and they have not found out how to turn their frustration into fuel for their destiny.

You can't allow your life experiences to change your expectations. It is very easy to fall into the swamp of *'this is how it always has been; no matter how hard I try, this is how it always ends up'.* I have often found that this comes from being weary in well-doing; because when you become weary of doing anything, you have the tendency to not to apply the same strength and effort that it takes for great things to come out of your life. If you have been like me, there has been times where I categorized the amount of strength and effort I put forth as "my best", but I was really only functioning on autopilot.

How to know when you're functioning on autopilot.
1. When you can function with no passion
2. When there is a set amount of effort
3. When you're not really concerned about the outcome
4. When you can only retain irritation and not information

Looking back now, I can honestly say I had it completely wrong. How much of my life had I actually wasted with this mind frame, with this illusion that I was actually giving "my best"? It wasn't my best at all. I'm sure that's the reason why I did not get noticed, or it wasn't a huge factor for my supervisor not to even mention me; now, it makes perfect sense. The majority of the time when I came through the door, I was always in a hurry to leave. I really didn't apply myself the way I could have; I thought I would get by with just enough, and in my mind, I would validate the lack of effort I applied on a day-to-day basis because I was not receiving what others got. But, assessing the situation, I now understand completely why I was overlooked. I came in moping and dragging and hating my life, while Aaron came in with the attitude that he was ready to work and get the job done.

Oh, yeah—and to finish the story, about three months later the company ended up acquiring a new contract, and the CEO specifically asked that Aaron oversee the project. All of this brings me to the conclusion that we have to honestly and sincerely evaluate what we consider our "best". Giving my best requires the maximum effort; small or big, I must give 110% in order to qualify my effort as <u>my</u> best.

The Valuable Me

We often enter into business agreements with the idea of what we can get out of it. This *is* something to be considered, but along with that, we need to understand the law of reciprocity. I believe that we are in a time and place where this principle isn't found in many people, because it's something that is not being taught nor its value understood. Looking back on the story I just shared, I ask myself, *was I really worth the amount of money I wanted?* I would have to say yes, according to my skill set—my ability to actually perform the task. On the other hand, I would have to say no because I did not apply myself; I did not give my best 'me'. I gave my supervisor the worn-out, unfocused, unmotivated, always-feeling-cheated, and complaining version of myself. I honestly did not understand the value of my position. My supervisor would always tell me positive things but it was very difficult for me to receive them, because I only equated *value* to *money* and I never measure the value of anything else. I can't believe how much time I spent walking around the place with the idea in my mind, *eventually, they'll fire me.* My mentality was contradictory: on one hand I wanted to be paid more money, but on the other hand I honestly admit that I was not a good employee. At that point I did not understand what had gone wrong; I loved the job, I loved the people—but now I realize I did not give them the best 'me'.

When you get to that perfect place and opportunity, you cannot afford to go into it detached from the task. Any time you do a task that you're not attached to, it can be tiring, and you become irritated about the responsibilities that have been allocated to you. That's why it's vitally important to evaluate where you are and what you're doing. When it comes down to doing what you do for a living, it has to be something that you're *called* to, and not just something you *like*. I have a God-given inspiration to do. Regarding some of the things that I do, at certain times I may not necessarily like the *process* but I am very passionate about the *outcome*. Your mind has to transcend what you like into what you're passionate about. If you ever plan on doing anything great, you're going to go through a season of discomfort, that is guaranteed; but the great thing in understanding this particular season is knowing that it's all part of a process that is going to bring you into greatness. So, I suggest you don't strive to be a *good* employee but rather strive to be the *greatest* employee—and that happens when you bring the most valuable you to your employers. That happens when:

1. **You're rested**
2. **Kind**
3. **Organized**
4. **Attentive**
5. **Passionate**

I am very sure that these things work. I am sure to the point that, even if you may not have all of the credentials you need for certain jobs, these principles and attributes that you have adapted to your character will either get you a second look at an interview, or a second look for evaluation for promotion. Job security comes from being indispensable; when I raise my level of self-value, I become irreplaceable to other people because I do the job so well.

I'm not a Placeholder

You must connect with your purpose in life if you're ever going to raise the value of the stock that's labeled 'me'. Passion transcends you from being a person with a position to an absolute 'must-have' in order for your vision to come into fruition. When you are Christian, having you on the team in any arena of life should be a plus and a benefit to the people you serve. To make this clearer, I tell you that you must have a passion for the problems of your supervisor/boss. Every job you ever got is because *somebody* had a problem—they needed to get something done that they couldn't do themselves, so they hired *you*.

Never allow yourself to be put in a position where people only view you as a placeholder until the real thing shows up. It's the same as the distinction between a temporary worker versus a full-time employee. A temporary worker does not get the same benefits as a full-time employee. The temp has access to the same places with some of the same tasks, takes on some of the same responsibilities, but does not receive the same benefits as a full-time employee. Another thing that will make you a placeholder is when you commit to doing only the minimum. It would be classified as insanity to invest the maximum into a person who's only willing to give you the minimum—and that does not come without conditions. "Just enough" or "this was all I could do" simply doesn't cut it.

You've got to be driven and motivated to bring another person's dream into reality if you work for them. One of the most important things to motivate you is that you have to see your part in it; you have to see yourself with the company. Even if it's a temporary position, you've still got to leave a good impression because you never know who will be empowered down the road of life.

The more you love what you do, the more people will love for you to do it. When you're passionate you can hold a place together; when you *lack* passion, you become a placeholder. You must understand that *nobody* will invest more in yourself than you will. Everyone that you work with should know that you are a good investment. What makes you stand out head and shoulders above anyone else is <u>character</u>. Good character is priceless in any arena whether it's in a relationship, the workplace, or even Church.

char·ac·ter / ˈkariktər/
The mental and moral qualities distinctive to an individual.

Character is one of the most overlooked things in relationships. For men, we often look for women who will do our bidding, with no questions asked. And for a large number of women, there's a certain criteria list a man has to meet in order for him to be considered a candidate for anything. Character is something that often goes under the radar, or is put neatly on the back burner as something we can get to later. We cannot allow this to happen, because character is one of the major things that will cause a marriage or relationship to self-destruct over time.

The fact of the matter is, a person can love you like no other has ever loved you in your life, and master the art of satisfying your physical needs—along with taking you on a sexual escapade that leaves you on Cloud Nine. And when all of that is over, their character will send you plummeting to earth in at an alarming speed because you only focused on them being into *you*, instead of taking the opportunity to examine *their character*. One of the things that I absolutely need to have is a relationship that is healthy, and by healthy I mean that both parties are receiving nourishing attributes that replenish each other.

If you're going to be married or date God's way, you have to get self-gratification out of the room and have the type of standards that cause you to evaluate things in the way that God would look at them.

1 Samuel 16:7 (NLT)
But the Lord said to Samuel, "Don't judge by his appearance or height, for I have rejected him. The Lord doesn't see things the way you see them. People judge by outward appearance, but the Lord looks at the heart."

In selecting anybody, you have to understand how they were *before* you or, better yet, *when you're not around*. In order to find this out you don't need to invest large sums of money into private investigators or ask somebody to snoop around for you. You have to pay attention to small details; it is those small details that allow us to get a glimpse of a person's character. There are millions of people who are heartbroken, not because of love, but because of character flaws that were overshadowed by the attention they always craved and the appreciation they felt they deserved. So lost in the utopia of emotions, we overlook character and pass it off by saying, "everyone has something they need to work on".

Though this statement is true, it would be in your best interest before connecting with anybody to know what they need to work on. For instance, if you are person who has to multitask every day—juggling family, work, and possibly other things—it will probably not be in your best interest to connect with somebody who has trust issues. Even though they may be devoted to you one hundred percent, they expect the same type of attention from you, no matter how you try to keep your focus on other things you are juggling. Insecurity falls on one of the greatest pillars of character, which is trustworthiness. We cannot take the world's definition of this because it is a selfish, one-sided view that causes you to question everybody else and subject them to unfair interrogation. Dealing with someone's insecurity is like dealing with extreme heat; you can become exhausted and depleted very quickly. Sometimes this is viewed as falling out of love, and honestly that's not always the case. We have made love this large canopy that's all-encompassing of emotions and character traits; but before you make it a circus where everything is under the big top, you need to understand that character is something independent of love. Though they can be a reflection of each other and can depend on each other, they are not exactly the same. Character is something that is built and shaped over time and has very little to do with the warm, fuzzy feelings of love. Character is something that is shaped when you first meet a person, not something you catch; it is something that has been instituted in you from when you were a child and built upon throughout your life, especially your teen years and earlier adulthood. It is built upon by your life experiences and also by the people who influenced you. You can always trace what a person knows back to the people who influenced them and built the foundational pillars of their personality; or who left them at a deficit and caused them to have character flaws.

In the initial stages it's easy to get carried away by the warm fuzzy feeling; but if you intend to have any type of real longevity with this person, you have to be attentive to their character in the beginning. Being blindsided by people's actions is always a struggle to process, and may tend to leave you scratching your head. That's why it's important to come into any relationship or agreement with a little bit of knowledge beforehand. Please don't get me wrong: love is absolutely important and for some it is easy to fall into. I've already been there, so I can honestly say that character is an important factor in whether a person stays or leaves from your life. So before you say 'I do' or 'I will', don't leave the box labeled 'character' unchecked. Having a good understanding may deflate the "I love you balloon" a little, but by applying this indispensable knowledge, you will thank me in the long run.

Now from a leadership standpoint....

Character is the defining point "where the rubber meets the road", as they say. It separates the mature from the immature. There are plenty of talented people, but very few of high character; so if you are an employer looking for an employee or vice versa, this is going to be that defining factor that will cast a different light on you.

It's not really difficult to find talented people in the world today, because information is so readily available. You can find teenagers with skills almost equal to traditional schooling and training; now, all they need is passion and the Internet and they're ready to compete with the best of them. But character is *not* a trait that can be learned over the Internet. You have to live your life under principles that are positive. Have you ever worked with somebody who was very talented and they were efficient at getting the job done, but when it came down to it they were very difficult to work with because of their character? Honestly, I have been on both sides of the fence; I have been the difficult person to work with and I've also been publicly sabotaged by someone else's character. It is great to have a passion to get certain things done but if you tear up so much in the process, you really have not accomplished anything. The first step to building your character is self-evaluation.

And you have to be honest!!!!!!

Taking consistent inventory of yourself allows you to make the necessary adjustments for the next level of your life. Always examine yourself. Some situations in life occur only to bring back your proper perspective, and this is important if you plan to raise your personal stock to make others want to invest in your leadership. The greatest co-worker you'll ever work with is the one whom you can trust and depend on. When you adjust your character, you set yourself up for your future. Character is important to have if you're going to lead people; you can be really gifted without it, but still frustrated because your character deflects everything and everybody that your gift attracts. I can think of the countless opportunities I have blown because of it; but after you have lost as many opportunities as I have, you draw some conclusions. The majority of bad attitudes I've ever had were due to character defects—something that I did not check within myself—so I misinterpreted the responses I was getting from people; I thought it was *them* and it was really *me*. So what I did is I began to look in the mirror and pick out things that I didn't like about myself—not in any self-condemning way, but in a way that allowed me to make adjustments to 'me'. Then, I began to see that it wasn't that people hated me, it was just that some of the things about my character were a turnoff.

Once I understood that, it was all uphill from there. The reason that I say 'uphill' is because there were certain situations I created myself that I had to deal with. I had to show the people that I was leaving with this bad impression that I was not the same person. That's right: leaders make mistakes. I don't care what facet of leadership that you're in, whether it's a business or whether it's a church, it's still the same—leaders make mistakes. A lot of times it's not that the leader is evil or mean, it's just that we still have character defects that we are trying to mature from—and very often, those things are not perfected in us until we take hold of a task.

One of the challenges of leadership is there are a lot of times where you have to do everything in public, and you have to function as though nothing is going on with you. You have to process your issues and problems in public; you have to deal with others' issues in public; and you still have to meet the needs of other individuals. Sometimes the stress of leadership causes you to want to revert back to your old habits, but you have to keep going in order to move into your destiny. With any level of success, there's going to be struggle. One of the easiest options is to simply give up and throw in the towel but after all you've been through, I'm sure that you're a little tougher than that; but sometimes the mental stress can be so bad that you actually entertain the thought. The truth of the matter is, it takes strength to maintain good character in front of people and you cannot let it take a nose dive in private. That's why it's important to pray; to have a secret place where you relieve your stress and draw your energy. It's the only way to hold these things in check and still operate in any level of leadership. You can't draw your strength from a public place, it has to be done in a secret place—a place that cannot be penetrated by the issues and problems of the place where you lead or the people you lead.

There's a certain level of discretion that every leader must have, which is the separation between those whom you lead and yourself. Don't get me wrong—this is not division; but if you're going to be a leader, don't expect for everybody to be present when you go through a process. Everybody cannot handle or fathom you being weak for even a moment, and that's why I say it's beyond dangerous to draw your strength from a public place. This will only hurt you in the long run because it's very difficult to recover when you have allowed a lot of people to be in your personal space. Today's vent can be tomorrow's venom. On the other side of things, love all transparency in leadership among your inner circle. I'm a strong believer that transparency can happen without losing integrity, and this only happens when there are people who are connected to your betterment. Their main concern is *you*—not necessarily what you're doing or what you have been. 'Equally yoked' is not necessarily a term just for marriage, but I think it's an all-encompassing term that allows us to not be desperate but more selective because of our situations. No matter if it's love or career, in this day and time we have to make smart choices. I believe one policy has to come back into our culture, and that is to be selective and have a standard. We can no longer live life as though the pains, shortcomings, disappointments, and struggles that we've dealt with in life are a legitimate excuse. No longer!!! This book is to get you ready to make great decisions and connect the right people with the right you. I believe that you are greater than you previously thought or expected, and the better life is right around the corner—once you move in the right direction.

> **GreenNote:** *Don't let your character defects deflect favor with people that God has given you!*

Chapter 6

The Three Rules of Connection

Before getting into anything, you have to have certain principles that you go by; you can no longer make decisions out of desperation.

I believe that there are three rules of engagement with anybody, and these rules are going to help you make great decisions. Not perfect decisions, but decisions that God is pleased with and you are proud of.

RULE #1 Never get into anything without expecting to show commitment

The reason why this is important is because when you connect with the right people, you still have to show a level of commitment no matter how circumstances start off. Things can start off very bleak and dark, and that has absolutely *nothing* to do with the agreement you've made. If you agree to do anything, you have to be committed to the end of the project. You can't get into the mindset that you're only in it to get something out of it. If you want to build successful relationships and make great decisions, you have to get rid of the 'pimp' mentality and go into the situation with the idea of being committed until the end; not just in the beginning, not just when things look good, but even when things gravitate to the worst. Your attitude must be, *'I can still be optimistic because I believe in the commitment that I made'*. You have to have a clear focus on the goal and expect the ups and downs. After proper assessment you should understand that there are no perfect situations, and after maturing into an adult you should understand that there are no perfect people. We all come from different backgrounds, different understandings, different ideologies, or impulses about life. But what makes a great connection is the ability to stay committed to the goal without being sidetracked by small things. Commitment happens when you come to the realization that you want something badly enough; that you're willing to commit to it even though it may not presently feel good; and you understand that it is a good decision that will pan out in the end. Looking at American history, all of the people who have done phenomenal things and created life-changing inventions have been through the wringers of disappointment and discouragement. If you have been a person like me, who gives up easily, this is the season of your life to be confident and committed to everything you do.

Sometimes I think that people just don't understand the power that lies behind commitment. It is not the same as enthusiasm; unfortunately, enthusiasm can wear off. A lot of times, it happens when the newness is gone or nobody gives the applause anymore and all the cheerleaders are gone. You have to rebuild the enthusiasm that has started to seep out like when a pin punctures a balloon. Through it all, there is a certain understanding that grows and a joy you feel at the end of a project, to know that you have gone through all phases of it, and you are finally finished.

If you're going to be committed, you have to work on your patience issues. We are often selfish because our perspective is mainly centered on our own comfort, not necessarily thinking about another perspective.

Are you that person sitting in traffic, screaming and agitated at people because they won't drive like *you* want them to? It's amazing how we come to the conclusion that they should be able to drive—even though we have no idea of the situation they're dealing with, nor know the mechanical issues with their vehicle; and what about that driver who suddenly becomes ill and needs medical attention? Along with these possibilities, there could also be other distracting factors going on. There are simply times in life when you have to be patient, and people often struggle with this because they are self-centered. In order to be committed all the way, you have to be patient. The lack of patience will cause you to always move out of sync and out of turn; I believe that one of Satan's greatest tricks is to get you to be impatient so you will miss the opportunity in business or the move of God in church that will allow you to advance your life to the next level. The agent of sabotage is impatience. If you knew the blessing that some things would yield in your life if you wouldn't allow waiting to get on your nerves, you would *be quiet and focus* instead of being disgruntled and complaining. Here's the small print: being patient can wear you down and deplete you sometimes, but the Scriptures say:

Isaiah 40:31 (New King James Version)

But those who wait on the Lord shall renew their strength; they shall mount up with wings as eagles, they shall run and not be weary, they shall walk and not faint.

So when you are patient, there will come a season of renewal and re-strengthening. You have to believe God more than you believe yourself, and absolutely trust His plan for your life—and know that this plan has a method of activation and commitment to the protocol required.

Now, on the other side of this coin, you can't over-commit yourself to a multiplicity of things. If you spread yourself too thin, you will never be able to concentrate your efforts in one place. It is the equivalent of inviting people to your house; telling them you're making sandwiches for everyone for lunch; then, to everyone's surprise you go into the kitchen to feed your hungry guests and you make one sandwich. You place your picture-perfect sandwich on a plate and cut it into multiple squares, intending to feed all your guests with that one sandwich; but everybody gives you the side-eye because they're surprised at what you're offering! Your response to them is "I think that's the best I can do"—and you're right. You used the best ingredients, you assembled it as if it belongs on a billboard; but the problem is *it's not enough for everyone to enjoy*—it's simply not enough to go around. It would have been better if you had just taken the time to commit to what you could do rather than trying to satisfy a lot of different people with only a limited amount of food. Metaphorically, this is how we often default our time to the things that we do. We put a lot of things on our plate, and we honestly get up every day with the intentions of doing our absolute best—but the lack of focus overshadows the effort, because of not being patient and committing to one thing. We spread ourselves too thin, and nobody gets enough to complete the task at hand. This creates frustration and even conflict, because you keep saying, *"I'm doing my best"* while the other party keeps saying, *"you're not doing enough"*. The only way this probably will be resolved is to sit down and commit to something; you have to break down the things you do, prioritize the things that are important, and delegate your efforts and time to places that are absolutely necessary to your purpose in life. If it has nothing to do with your purpose, it should have nothing to do with you;

you have no time to waste on purposeless time traps that only subtract from your valuable time and effort and take you in a direction that you are not even going. Quite frankly, you cannot promise everybody the moon, because you cannot deliver the moon to everybody—you are a limited resource. You are a limited commodity. You cannot be spread all across the globe and expect to be effective everywhere. You have to know your purpose in life and make decisions based on your purpose—and once these decisions have been made, you have to stick to them.

Commitment causes you to stand the test of time, despite the odds, oppositions, and frustrations. If you make any type of agreement with anyone, you have an understanding that you are in it for the long haul. As I said in the beginning, you have to count up the cost and after you have made your decision, you have to hang in there in spite of the difficulties.

No shortcuts

Philippians 4:6-7 (New King James Version)
Be anxious for nothing, but in everything by prayer and supplication, with thanksgiving, let your requests be made known to God; and the peace of God, which surpasses all understanding, will guard your hearts and minds through Christ Jesus.

Being committed and still retaining your motivation causes you to think and operate on another level that transcends the comprehension of others around you. Whenever you become committed to something, you'll always have people around you who wonder or question why you do what you do—which is something you have to be totally okay with. You'll never get to the end of anything or succeed at anything without having <u>critics</u> and <u>criticism</u> that you'll endure. In order to get a diamond, you've got to start from the coal process. With your new mind and new focus, you have to take the criticism of your skeptics and use it as fuel.

Just because you're committed to something, it does not mean you will have a bandwagon of cheerleaders even if it is for something good. And just because you don't have a support system, it does not give you the excuse to take the easy route. There will be a period in life where you have to simply wait patiently and ignore what's going on around you, because once you pay attention to those things you'll try to start looking for an easy way out to ease the social and mental conflicts. This is the reason why you have so many people who have forfeited their own destiny: to stop being the topic of other people's conversation, and to defuse the ridicule they've taken on for having the audacity to be committed to something that may not be popular. I want to encourage you by saying there is a due season that is coming because you have the audacity to hold on to hope even in the midst of hell. To bypass the shortcuts, you have to stay focused on your goal. If your goal is to be promoted on your job, you have to bypass the opportunity to 'get over' on your boss by becoming a lazy employee. If you want a loving, fulfilling marriage you have to bypass opportunities to disrespect, get even, or fall into stubbornness and secrecy; commitment is universal, across-the-board.

We're living in a time where loyal people are almost an endangered species, and longevity is something that is almost unheard of. Listening to an interview of a very popular Hip Hop artist the other day, I heard him make a very staggering statement. He said that the longevity of music is no longer relevant in the business; that there used to be a time where, if you had a hot song, it lasted a long time. He even said that there was a time when you played a hot song in the club from last year, people would get up and say *"that's my jam"*. But now, he says people don't take the time to listen to good music. They listen to it, and then they are on to the next one. What I gathered from this interview is that, culturally, we're drifting into a 'microwave' society that does not take the time to develop anything or properly produce anything. As believers, we can't fall into that trap. Anything worth having or of value requires a certain level of development and production. You can't kick and scream because something is not picture-perfect or exactly what you want. With your relationships of any kind, there has to be a period of development and production. You can't be in a hurry to leave because it's not what you want. My philosophy is if you want oranges or if you want apples, you have to plant seeds and grow them. Anybody can jump on the bandwagon or steal somebody else's tree because:

1. They don't want to pay the cost for the seed
2. They don't want to pay that much attention to the development process

Any time the development process has been tampered with, you can rest assured that there will be unnecessary compromises in the end, because you were not committed to the process. So no matter what process, be committed to the outcome.

Rule #2. Perspective "Looking Forward".
What you think is what you get! (Proverbs 23:7)
How am I looking at the situation I'm entering?

Is this agreement something I can actually maintain?
What am I looking to gain?
What am I looking to give?

These are all questions you need to ask yourself before entering into any type of agreement, personal or public. You have to understand the power of agreement. When you agree to something, the understanding should be that we have similar values, similar views, and we're both working towards the same goal.

Having a clear understanding and entering into any agreement is a necessity for success. Nobody has a successful marriage by accident, and nobody becomes the CEO of a company by chance. Nobody starts their own business without having clear intentions. I believe that God allows life to bring us a variety of things, and we have the ability to call it a curse or a blessing. Your perception is evident in what you call it; are you always looking at things as an *obstacle* or an *opportunity*? A building block or stumbling block? Your perception has to be based on the power of God that lies within you to do the thing that you are doing. Where we seem to fall into trouble is when we try to calculate things on our human ability without depending on Him; contrary to what people may think or believe, we were built to be dependent upon Him. He is the Sovereign Ruler in sovereign authority over all life, and we have to trust Him.

First, you have to understand His perception of you so that you can properly understand the perception He wants you to have. The only way anybody ever gets you to change your perception is when you identify your purpose. If you never identify your purpose, you will never change your perception. When you find your purpose it almost becomes second nature to be committed to it. And from purpose we cast our perception. Simply ask somebody about their purpose; if they can't tell you their sole purpose for existing, I can almost guarantee you they can't tell you what direction their life is headed in. For us Christians who cannot answer this question, we use either of these two statements:

"My life is in the Lords hands" or "I go wherever God leads me".

Though I agree to both statements, neither one of them answers either of the previous two questions. One thing is certain about God's nature—it is consistent. Everything that God created serves a purpose and solves a problem.

Let's look at the dependency between plants and animals.

Plants give off O2 and sugar, which the animals need to survive, and they in turn give off CO2, which the plants need.

As we can see in creation, God creates *everything* with a purpose, so that includes you. Once you tap into your purpose, your perception begins to take shape with your destiny in view. Just one taste of your purpose will make you change; decisions you once hailed as absolute truths become things of the past, because you had a glimpse of your destiny. It makes you step out with nothing to step on. That's why you have to make sure that your perception is clear and 100% in every decision that you make.

In this day and time you have to make sure that every time you connect with somebody, you have an understanding of their perception of *you* and *them*. Not understanding this in the beginning of connections can cause us to be unequally yoked down the line; then, frustration is inevitable when gray areas are present. Even from the perspective of friendship: no matter how long you've known a person or how long they previously knew you, your changed perception may make people feel uncomfortable with the new you. If you have to compromise the steps that you have taken in your life in order to make them feel comfortable where they are, maybe you should evaluate whether you should be with them. Going into any situation you have to be optimistic, because there will be shortcomings, disagreements, and flaws with any human being on the planet. You have to look at yourself for a solution; when God puts two of anything together, they fit together perfectly.

Purpose and Position

These are two things that you have to keep in perspective: purpose and position. In order for me to be effective in any relationship of any nature, I have to know my *purpose*. Then I have to look at how my purpose lines up with the *position* that I have now joined. If I take a position that doesn't line up with my purpose I'll be doing things out of ritual, and my heart will not be in it. This is evident; if there's a job, you have the person who races to do things just to say they're done, versus the person who comes early, leaves late, and does whatever their task is *passionately* because it pains them to see something not done to perfection. They go to great lengths to get the job done, and receive no credit for it just to know that is done. That's how important and attractive it is when a person works on something that's not just a position, but a purpose passion.

Purpose passion is something that I defined as:

Something that God has instinctively put inside of you that is activated and pulled out of you when you enter into anything that lacks your God-given ability.

Positional inspiration is:
Fulfilling a task only because you have the position, and only exercising the authority that comes along with the position because it provides some form of self-gratification.

There is no passion, no drive, and no eagerness to learn how to perfect what they do, because their mindset is simply, *'I have to go ahead and get this out-of-the-way'*. Anything a person is passionate about, he never wants to just get it out of the way— he wants some more of it. When your perception is connected to your purpose, there is a certain sense a fulfillment when you are operating in a position. Not having your purpose connected to your perception can make you feel overworked, because what you do every day for five days out of the week can be bland and dull; you will always find yourself frustrated because this is something that, in your heart of hearts, you really don't want to do. You can have a positive outlook on something that you view as being dull. Save the weeks, months, and years of frustration by consulting God first.

Projecting your perspective from your purpose allows you to access the appropriate relationships based on your destiny and not just your circumstance in life. Why, you may ask? Circumstances *will* and always *do* change your perspective, in order to stay intact when life's ups and downs occur.

Rule #3 Clean Slate

Acts 3:19
New Living Translation (NLT)
Repent therefore and be converted, that your sins may be blotted out, so that times of refreshing may come from the presence of the Lord,

This is absolutely true when it comes down to salvation, but I believe this can be applied as a principle in other areas of life as well. I think it's important that we understand our mistakes instead of suppressing and hiding them. After all, failure is only an opportunity to readjust and reapply the right application for success. Some failures in life are attributed to the directions we have followed; however, as long as you have life in your body you have the opportunity to start over again. So don't worry about the things you lost in previous times—this is a new day and a new season. It's time to turn from your old directions and choose a higher path. In your old life, you made decisions out of desperation; in your new life you make decisions out of destiny, and if you're going towards your destiny you can't be hung up on your past.

It might sound like a cliché, for you've heard it 1 million times, but I want to tell you that there is so much waiting for you on the other side; but you first have to make a complete U-turn on life's highway. A lot of times, we don't go in the right direction because we have settled for the existence that we're living. We have defused our dreams and we have assassinated our aspirations because of failures, and over time, replaying this again and again in your mind can become a prison. When you have the opportunity to start a new relationship, agreement, or partnership with somebody, after a time it may start to feel to them as though they're visiting a person in a mental jail cell with sporadic visiting hours. It's like they're talking to you through a glass; they see you, can actually physically touch you—and as bad as they want to have a real relationship with you, you're still stuck behind the glass window for a crime done long ago. You're still mentally paying the price for that crime.

Then, there's the person who has done a lot of wrong things in their life to try to wash away the pain of somebody who has either manipulated them, or did not understand what it took to have a relationship with them. So now they walk around with a chip on their shoulder that nobody sees or knows of, because that part of their life has been dumped into "Area 51" and cannot be found. It's like they use military-grade armed security so that you will not dig up areas of their past.

Personally, I learned that it was largely my own fault that got me into some of the greatest struggles and shortcomings that I've ever experienced in my life. This kind of realization may cause two things to happen. First of all, you may be in a bind mentally, and feel like you can never completely shake it. Secondly, whatever happened may make you bitter towards people that you feel have misused you or mishandled the relationship with you; either way, it is still like living in a prison. The way that you get out of this mindset is by converting your thoughts.

Philippians 4:8
New King James Version (NKJV)
Finally, brethren, whatever things are true, whatever things are noble, whatever things are just, whatever things are pure, whatever things are lovely, whatever things are of good report, if there is any virtue and if there is anything praiseworthy— meditate on these things.

In the society that we live in, our minds are under constant attack, to the point that we find ourselves unknowingly acting out things that we have seen. Wanting to change is one thing, but actually putting forth the effort to make the necessary adjustments to change—and stick to those changes—is something totally different. The Bible shows us exactly what to think if we are going to be successful; to have a life of less stress and more harmony between you and the people in your life, you have to be committed to the conversion process in order to see change and success.

From a church standpoint, it amazes me that this topic is not emphasized and hammered home, because this is where so many people are tripped up. Without committing to the conversion process, you'll be trying to stuff old concepts into a renewed mind and eventually you'll say, *"it does not work"* and revert back to your old self.

Once your mind has been renewed, you have to grasp new concepts. So many opportunities that God has planned for all our lives come around quickly, but what hinders us from going forward and processing these things is our refusal to turn from the old mindset. If you want the best out of a relationship, marriage, friendship, or family, you have to start all over again with a clean slate—and *don't* drag old things into a new environment.

Chapter 7

Wedding day fine print

Dearly beloved, we are gathered here today, **UNDER** the sight of God to **Join** this Man and Woman in **HOLY MATRIMONY.**

Before you pick out the *"OMG! This is it Dress"* or plan the bachelor Party that no one will ever fully remember, let's go through the fine print of marriage that so many seem to miss out on.

If marriage between a man and woman was God's idea, we must seek Him first before buying the rings. We must have a clear-cut understanding of God's principles about marriage. To properly understand this union between you and the love of your life, you must start at the origin of marriage. The single most important thing about marriage is that it's under the principles and authority of God, and Him alone.

Contrary to popular belief, marriage was never intended to be redefined by man on is functionalities or its participants. "Gathered under the sight of God" is such a powerful statement. Think about it; you are under somebody who knows all and sees all. He knows the intentions of your heart, there is no secret thing that is hidden from His eyes. I know that we may live in a different time now, but there was once a time when, in order to marry a person, you had to go through their parents. Their parents had to know you; and, in thinking about it, shouldn't it still be the same way? If you're going to pledge a life that God has given you to someone, shouldn't they be known by our Heavenly Father? And, no!—going to church when you were a kid and could barely remember it does not count. I'm talking about having a *personal relationship* with God—not defined by your own terms, but a life centered and focused on the will of God.

Truthfully, marriage is full of different twists and turns. Ups and downs are inevitable, but through those difficult times you have to remember how love responds and displays itself in times of conflict and trouble. Marriage cannot be fueled by one's selfish ambitions or desires, but we must show God our accountability through a submitted life under fire and pressure.

The scripture says in the book of Psalms 91:1

He who dwells in the secret place of the Most High shall abide <u>UNDER</u> the shadow of the Almighty.

The secret place is found only when you submit to God in real worship. Adam was a worshiper before he was a husband and because he was a worshiper, God saw that man needed a helpmate; a counterpart of himself, one formed from him, and a perfect resemblance of his person.

We must understand that the things we are looking for are connected to our ability to stay under God. It is the one principle that alters the results of marriage. Anytime you take something from under God's umbrella, you are subject to the outside forces of life. We must put first things first and realize that we are together **UNDER** the sight of God, so He sees all of us—inward and outward—and we are held accountable for how we have taken care of our spouse. Think about it, everything that God gives you comes with instructions. **UNDER** God's divine order there is God's law, and if we are under God we must follow His instructions. We can't get into marriage with the idea that it's just me and my spouse, but in fact it's God too. We must have the mindset that I am in authority and **UNDER** authority.

Trust that God's plan for marriage is happiness, not a living hell. God's idea of marriage is far beyond what our natural minds can conceive. His ways are definitely not our ways, and His thoughts are definitely not our thoughts. He knows exactly what we need, that's why He requires complete submission. Until you submit to Him, you'll always have problems accessing the full benefits of God's plan of marriage. We absolutely have to change our understanding of marriage. Some of the things we see pertaining to marriage equate it to a jail cell or prison sentence—and it is completely *not* God's idea of marriage, which is beautiful and holy, and right in the sight of God. God never meant for man to stray away from His central theme. LOVE is the driving force behind everything that God does, so quite naturally His first institution would be built on it.

Amos 3:3
New Living Translation (NLT)
Can two people walk together without agreeing on the direction?

The Mash Potato Lesson

Before you say "I do", you must take the necessary time to understand your mate's standards on the important issues. Very little changes about how a person feels about major issues, and we cannot change a person. Now that you are joined, one of the biggest fights you will encounter is the bout between uncompromised personalities. Refusal to compromise is like igniting the fuse on a stick of dynamite: nobody wins after the smoke clears. No matter how much you feel like you're right—and that the only thing that needs to happen is for your mate to listen to you—a compromise still has to be made. If the Bible says:

Romans 12:10
New Living Translation (NLT)
Love each other with genuine affection, and take delight in honoring each other.

Philippians 2:3
New Living Translation (NLT)
Don't be selfish; don't try to impress others. Be humble, thinking of others as better than yourselves.

You have to change your mindset, if you're going to be married God's way. You can't use marriage as a means to get what you always wanted in life. It can't be self-serving and it cannot fill voids for what happened in childhood. Your mate cannot be your personal verbal punching bag, nor can you make them pay for something they didn't even do.

You can run into some difficult hurdles—nothing in life worth keeping comes without challenge, or absent of struggle. But what will frustrate any marriage is when you plan to start your new life together but fail to mention the things connected to you that *you* can't let go, or that don't want to let go of *you*. These include ties to people from the past, belief systems, family bonds, financial philosophies, sexual appetite, spending habits, and children.

Relinquishing authority can be one of the most difficult things you face in the beginning years of marriage. *Why do you say that,* you ask? Because if you've been the boss for 20 or 30 years, there can be some very difficult challenges with simply getting out of the driver's seat, or considering someone other than yourself because you're not single anymore.

One of the most dangerous mindsets to come into marriage with is a 'single' one. If you are set on staying single in your thought process, you inadvertently plan to shoot your marriage down out of the sky. The quest to become one flesh is not a lightweight job; Genesis tells us that we must restructure our old life for the new one.

(Genesis 2:24) *Therefore a man shall leave his father and mother and be joined to his wife, and they shall become one flesh.*

These two are one flesh, they shall be considered as one body, having no separate or independent rights, privileges, cares, concerns, etc., each being equally interested in all things that concern the marriage state. Who God has joined together, let no issues from the past; or complications in the present; or difficulty in the future separate you from your mate.

To be joined means: to connect, to have a willing interest in learning how your mate works. Knowing their rhythms will stop you from putting expectations on them that can lead up to frustration. Joining is a very serious thing; it is fusion of two worlds that may have some issues with people, places, or things that already existed in your single life. Ties are some of the hardest things to break, especially when families are on the other end of the rope. Sometimes, family can be adamant about reminding you of all the wonderful times in the past and what they've done for you; but you cannot be enslaved to them for the rest of your life, because you are *joined* with someone who changes your priority list.

The more you understand this, the easier it will be to cut the cord and leave the nest. Too much reminiscing is bad for a healthy relationship; between you and your loved one, marriage is about building, not sightseeing.

To be joined in marriage means the two operate as **Dual-Singular.** This means that even though we may not be around each other, we still function and operate as though we are standing right next to one another. Even though we are different individuals, we can still function as one.

One of the greatest illustrations of this that I've ever seen is the process of making mashed potatoes:

1# You get two potatoes.
2# You skin them both.
3# You put both of them in a pot of boiling water.
4# The heat breaks down their texture.
5# Then, you take a utensil and mash them.
6# Mash until you see one heap of mashed potatoes.

Even though this sounds like a contradiction, it is absolutely essential to keep the harmony between you and your spouse. Ties to family or even a past life can be very detrimental to the growth of any marriage. This is not to imply that you should completely give up all contact, but you have to have a clear-cut boundary for your family if you're going to stay married. Anytime boundaries intersect into marriage, they can become blurred and people can misconstrue where the limitations are.

If you have family that's very protective of you before marriage, it is wise to listen to their counsel and take the opportunity to have a fresh eye to view certain aspects of your relationship. This council should come from somebody who is wise and not bitter about their own relationships. The danger in listening to bitter people is, they draw everybody into their mind frame. Just because we may go through the same thing does not mean we have the identical thinking process or response; different responses prompt different outcomes, and all truths are not transferable. The Bible is full of timeless, universal truths that will help you navigate through the rugged terrain of life.

So, to fortify the bond that you have, it's best to pray that God sends wise people into your life, because they're the best people to talk to when you are lost.

Add water and stir

Coming together as a family can present you with challenges that you didn't see coming. You can love someone dearly and they can be the love of your life, but what do you do when you have family and children that come along? It is a fact that you cannot ignore; it cannot be swept under the rug, you cannot be in hiding in another room—you have to deal with the rest of the family. You can't be joined to anybody and exclude their family. The reason why this is not healthy to do is because there are certain principles and understandings you need to grasp through exposure to your new family's environment. By excluding your mate's family, you don't get a chance to see some of the ideologies they have been exposed to which, in turn, are now introduced into your house—or, better yet, your family. Have you ever been part of a family and experienced some reluctance from either the children or the immediate family and you've felt as though they hated you or did not like you? You and your spouse may have become one flesh, but it may take some time to get the children and the immediate family on board, and that comes with patience and prayer. Though every situation is not the same, it takes a serious level of communication and love to function together as a family. It is important that everyone understands this if you want the best results out of your family. Everybody desires peace at home, because when you have peace at home it stops you from putting unnecessary pressure on outside relationships. It gives you a place of serenity and a place to refuel from the unexpected changes of life. This is achieved with clear communication, and taking the time to go the extra mile in love and in patience. When a person is introduced into a family it changes the whole equilibrium of the household, and there will absolutely be no peace without making adjustments. You can't take a family or go into any family 'as is', you have to come in with the idea that you are all going to work together to create harmony.

Children sometimes have the idea that you may be coming to take the place of their mother or father but if they perceive your care as an impeachment of their parent, they will be willing to fight you to the end. A subsequent mistake in this process is when you become frustrated and attempt to go in with force, which is a bad idea if you plan on winning them over. What you have to do is go away, and into prayer; take time to listen, and if you listen well enough, you can find the open door to a great relationship with the children that are now your family.

The institution may be under attack and the definition may be misdirected by circumstance, but God is still very serious about family. Before one place of worship was ever brought into existence, we saw the very character and nature of God's love through family. Take the time to build your family with the type of love that flows from heart-to-heart. As water is to a human, love is to a family—you simply can't survive without it.

Complete not Compete

This may sound like a misprint in the book, but when it comes down to relationships—and especially marriage—this is something that critically needs to be addressed. Opposition in life is inevitable. There's no way to avoid it, and I think anyone who is trying to move their life to the next level and make it better knows that we can't avoid it. But what do you do when the greatest opposition you face comes from the person who sleeps next to you in bed? It begins to weigh on the relationship, whether you address the issue or not. Time after time, moment after moment, the momentum of anger begins to build because you don't understand why this person is not your biggest cheerleader. This is more than friendly fire; this can feel like downright treason, and it can bring so much confusion into a relationship.

A lot of times, relationship have both complications and competitions. Because we don't take the time to explain in detail some of the ventures that we want to institute in our families, it creates miscommunication; your family may not completely understand the role that you have signed them up for. Then, out of miscommunication comes reluctance—they follow you and do things just because you've asked, completely devoid of the passion or drive that you may have. And because they may not see the full picture up front, they don't see it coming together. They will often try to divert energy and time into something else. Then, the competition starts; you find yourself working harder—not to complete the task, but to show them that they are wrong about what you're doing, *and* that they are wrong for not helping you. When we have children involved, the children can become part of a tug-of-war that will leave any house divided. When competing on jobs, places of worship, beliefs, direction, time expenditure, authoritative decisions, you end up looking back and wondering where did all the time go. Competitions drained the very life out of the relationship; you were never meant to *compete* with the person that God has given you, you were meant to *complete* them. When it comes down to any decision, it should be made equally—right down the middle; and if there is an executive decision that needs to be made on the spot, that decision has to be made with the other person in mind. We can't drift into selfish ambitions. Let's take a minute and look at the words Side by side:

Compete   Complete

What's the difference between these two words? You guessed it: the **L**. Just like this one letter changes the whole outlook and definition of the word, that's exactly how love changes our pursuit of everything in life. So, if you're eager to do anything, consult your spouse first—give them details, details ,details so they will not be blindsided and feel the need to take cover from this bombardment of confusing actions. You want people to follow you and help you because they believe in the purpose of God in your life. From my own personal experiences, simply asking *"How do you feel about this?"* would've saved me so much trouble and heartache. Now I realize I was making decisions too quickly, without fully thinking things through; and I didn't want to talk to her about it because I knew she would ask a million questions that I *wasn't* prepared to answer, but *should* have been. So, a secret decision resulted in public shame because we simply were not ready to make a decision that big. In an attempt to cover my pride, we ended up competing, and arguing about surface issues when the *real* issue was my pride.

Killer Competitors

It's a dangerous thing to be connected to somebody who feels that you are their competition. This is a very dangerous environment in which to live, work, or be in a relationship. If you're going to be **joined**, neither party can have the idea that beating the other person is the primary goal. Killer competition, in most cases, results from a person feeling as though someone's going to take their spotlight. Competitors sometimes stalk you like prey, and they dig up all the information they can find about you—just to have a juicy work conversation at the water cooler about you. Sadly, a lot of people in the workplace have the idea that we can't make it as a team; they think, *I can only make it by myself.* In some cases, being your brother's keeper has drifted into being your brother's killer. A lot of times, this happens when people are misguided about the source of their strength and appreciation. You abuse things when you try to get more out of them than what they promise; a job never promises to correct esteem issues or make you feel important. Actually, the only thing a job promises is pay and benefits, so your confidence cannot be predicated on what you do; it has to be squarely on what you believe. Missing this principle will cause you to misconstrue friendships and possibly abuse good people out of the fear of them taking your place. When the source of your strength comes from your job you will begin to shoot people down because of them doing well. In your mind, you're interpreting this as *you* losing ground, and you would do anything to get the affirmation of peers or superiors to gain favor with them. Have you seen one of those reality shows, where everybody is manipulating everybody else to come out as the winner? What happened to the good old days of winning things fair and square? When manipulation and treachery becomes normal behavior and doing what is right seems to be a foreign concept, we are drifting into a dangerous place. Envy and jealousy can be the driving force behind a person's actions. We clearly see this in the story of Cain and Abel; for instance, God tells Cain, "will you not be rewarded if you do well?" This is a clear indication that we cannot gauge our success on another person, because I sincerely believe that if Cain had done the right thing with his offering, God would have blessed him just as he did Abel.

It is not advisable to enter into any type of agreement with a person who is secretly envious over something you do or something you have.

Don't give out spare keys to your house

There are very simple ways to defuse any major issues down the line. Stop making your mate look attractive to other people! So now you're probably scratching your head, wondering what I am talking about. Well, it is very simple. There's a certain vibe you give off when you're unhappy; some way, somehow, it makes people who weren't previously attracted to you sympathize with you. That sympathy may then turn into comfort. This can lead to a breakdown of moral defense, which could ultimately lead to a compromise. When you're in the happy stages of love, it is easy to defend against all predators because when you're happy your lover is the object of your attention and the apple of your eye. But I think what Paul wrote in 1 Corinthians Chapter 3 is also applicable to your relationship, in that it will be tried by fire. Without question, if you plan to be with somebody for a long period of time there is a series of tests that time brings, and you have to stand those tests in order to have a healthy and long-lasting relationship. These things do not come overnight; it is through the happy times and the rigorous, hard times that we are refined into the people that you see celebrating their 50 year wedding anniversaries.

Side Chicks and Sugar Daddies work harder!

As bad as I hate to admit it, we're living in a world today where people will work harder to break apart relationships and marriages for their own selfish ambitions and because they cannot constrain themselves from the lust of their flesh. They will purposely go after something that is not theirs for the idea of self-gratification. How they catch their prey is to find individuals who are overworked, stressed and depressed, lonely, and confused. What makes them so attracted to your mate is the fact that they don't have to go into itemized detail about anything; they're really just there to listen for particular key phrases so they'll know which way to break down their defense—and most of the time, this action is disguised as 'help'. Sometimes they will engage in conversations and have no intentions at all of fulfilling anything that they've said. All they want is to satisfy the appetite of the flesh—the magic moment of compromise (sex). The more entertaining they are, the more they are psychologically breaking down your thought processes—to the point that you will eventually compromise. And Satan will put you in a conducive environment, causing you to look at what you have at home as unimportant; you'll start using your partner's flaws as the primary excuse, and compromise it all for the thrill and excitement of something new. This is a trap—don't fall for it! If you follow God's way and His plan, He will give you the desires of your heart, but Satan will only give you the desires of your flesh. He always offers a quick train ticket to paradise—with the price tag of denying God's principles and standards.

> **GreenNote:** *After the wedding day is over and the remaining slices cake is in the garbage, the honeymoon is now a memory the marriage begin. You are now joined*

Chapter 8

"Sex" Give it to me your way

Sex

It's best to tell the truth at this particular juncture in time; I believe that it's safe to say, ladies, that having sex with a man will not keep him. There is a great possibility that many men are not thinking of long-term relationships.

This is the result of a variety of backgrounds and deeply-embedded philosophies that are completely different from yours. It's important to have an understanding of a person's background, but this does not mean you should put on scuba gear to dive into a lot of things from the past. It's safe to have some understanding about a person philosophies, though; but that doesn't mean every horrific incident in this person's past will be repeated because, the fact of the matter is, a lot of us learn from our mistakes. Some of our mistakes, we will never, ever repeat because of maturity; but sadly, that is not the case for all of us.

Why is his sex so good?

When God made man in his own image He made him with sex in mind. Sex was something God had already configured into human existence so that it would ultimately be the portal of life. It was God's plan for the seed of Adam to perpetuate throughout all history, and everything that was spoken in Adam, according to Genesis 1:26. So with all this creative energy and authority that has been given to the males, it is safe to say that sex is almost more spiritual than it is physical. Sex can be like a car: it can be driven legally, or it can be driven illegally.

Do you remember the thrill of sneaking out of the house and driving your parents' car without their permission? Even though we knew it was wrong, it was still an adrenaline rush to drive the car without their permission—to do something you really wanted to do. It may have been about going somewhere specific, just riding around with your friends, or showing off to the people that didn't like you so well; but the fact was, after all of the excitement of showing off was over, you still had to deal with the drive back home. Everybody knows what that feeling is like: praying, wishing and hoping that you won't be caught, when in fact you should have just waited and gotten permission to drive the car in the first place. All of the worries would have been eliminated, and you'd have had way more fun. There is a certain type of protection that you are under when you get permission first. When you do something illegally, you are on your own. That protection is not there. You are subject to whatever happens, and whatever consequences come along with your actions.

Sex is ten times better when you have God's permission. Since it was His idea, it would be better if we followed His guidelines. It is best to wait for the right opportunity, ask for permission, put the key into the ignition and go for the ride of your life; rather than taking advantage in the heat of the moment and regretting it immediately or even years later. We are living in a time where we must be more conscious of our decisions and plans. Yes, I am telling you to **_plan a good sex life_**. We must stop leaving God out of intricate parts of life, since it was His idea in the first place. Why sneak into it at all? Why don't we take the time to incorporate Him into it, instead of being in a quagmire when it's not going right?

I sincerely believe that one reason why sex is so pleasurable is because it's a spiritual act as well as a physical act. Sex is so important that, even with a wedding, cake, rings, wedding party and honeymoon, if you got a divorce in a very short period of time, the judge wouldn't ask about any of that; he would ask if you <u>consummated</u> the marriage. Amazingly, the word consummate *means "to make a marriage legally complete and fully valid by having sexual intercourse"*. So that means sex was given to us for <u>purpose</u> and not just for pleasure.

Becoming one flesh

Yes it is true—the wedding dress, rings, tuxedos, flower girls and the rice all are good; but without sex, it is just an event. If sex is this important, we must take a good, thorough investigation of it from many perspectives. The first thing for us guys to scratch off the list is, sex is not a way to prove whether we still have it or not. We spend billions of dollars a year on male enhancement and stamina-increasing products to ensure that we are still running in tip-top shape. There are people who need these products for medical issues, not ego issues. But if we would tell the truth, the reason why this is a billion-dollar industry is because we men judge our performance based on vocal response and body movements; that's why in most cases, ladies, a man will ask *"Do you like that, is it good to you?"* Why does he ask you this? Very simple: men are inherently conquerors. It is intricately stitched into our DNA to be the winner; every man wants to feel like he's the king of the castle.

Ladies, it may all seem physical, but contrary to popular belief, it is not. Think about it—every time that you were ever cheated on, it was initiated by a good conversation, and in most cases the other woman was not just talking about how good he was in bed, she also injected his ego with a boost of confidence. Ladies, don't let your man suffer from ED. I am not talking about 'erectile dysfunction'; I am talking about 'ego deflation'. In the same way that you have days when you may not feel as pretty and beautiful as you are, there days that he has when he does not feel like the man he believes he is—or the man he thinks you need. It is important that you understand that, contrary to how a man acts, there's a part of him that is somewhat like a balloon. Once you inflate a balloon to its maximum capacity it looks really good, it's enjoyable, and it is a symbol of celebration; but what do you do when you see the balloon deflating? In this type of crisis, don't make the mistake of making yourself the source of his supply. Here's the truth: as good as he says your sex is, your sex will not solve any issues, pay any bills, or resolve any problems. When your relationship is centered on sex, you will have no clue how to deal with it when a major issue comes up.

Three things that Sex is Not!

Sex is not medication.

It will not numb you from realities and truths of either unresolved issues or future conflicts based on present decisions.

Sex is not an eraser.

It will not erase issues and mistakes. It was never created or intended to be the solution to man's problems. If that were so, every time we'd have a major issue we could all just rip off our clothes, jump in the bed, and everything would be okay; but for us, that's like living in the twilight zone. We know that it is not so. It takes time, effort and work to have a successful relationship.

Sex is not man-made, It's God Designed.

It is not however you want it or whenever you want; this is a portal into your spirit that allows you to become one with one another. And because Satan knows this, he uses this to destroy man and cause us to fall *Note that, in the Bible when the children of Israel fell, sexual immorality was often a part of it, and they fell into slavery to another nation.*

Number 25:1-3,   2 Kings 17:16-20

Because this is the act of bringing another life into the world, He demands that it be done His way, through marriage.

Back to the balloon.

To salvage the relationship that's in the marriage, it takes more than sex. For any man on the face of the planet, the word of a woman is like Helium. *Girl, don't you know that female affirmation is like the world's strongest drug, hands-down?* Ladies, you have the power of nurturing just by your words. A man will go to work all week long; work overtime; and come home exhausted on Friday just so you'll know and acknowledge that *he is the provider*. And we remember *what you say* that fuels us; to know that your woman appreciates you is like winning a trophy every day.

Free MILK!

It is statistically proven that a large number of relationships that begin with pre-marital sex end up in separation because of different philosophies about relationships **and** sex.

I believe that we must understand what a woman means when she 'gives in'. Men, in many cases you become "serious" because *she* understands that when she gives her all, she's not playing; she is not doing this for recreation, and she does expect appreciation—to the point that you should respect her silent wishes and become monogamous. The fact of the matter is, *everything* has a cost. When it comes down to sex, the reality is that men and women have two different ideas of how things should go in the bedroom.

For Christians, premarital sex can never be the answer to keeping the person you love in your life, and under no circumstances can we compromise. I know that we are living in the world, where everything is sexually influenced. Even commercial ads about toothpaste are now sexually attractive to the audience; the fact of the matter is, the world is using sex for *everything*. Can we really be surprised? After all, one of the most famous slogans in Hollywood is "sex sells"; but as Christians we still have to be convinced that God has a reward for those who diligently, wholeheartedly and radically go after Him. So, if He knows everything about us, why would you think your sex drive is not included? When God gives you a mate He doesn't leave any aspect out; that person will be cut to the continuity of your needs.

Chapter 9
Getting ready for church

The house of the Lord is a place where everybody is welcome and everybody should come. "Come as you are" is a statement that we have often said to people who are seeking hope, understanding, and God's love.

Don't get me wrong: I am not disputing this statement, but I think it's important that we understand the 'fine print' that, hopefully, is made clear in this chapter. No, I'm not a church expert. I don't have all of the answers; but I have been saved since I was thirteen years old, and there are some things I've learned that I want to share with you.

Right off the top, let's deal with what *not* to expect when you step foot into any church:

1# The church is full of people on different levels of faith and understanding, it's a learning process for them as well.

2# There is no guarantee that two different churches will be identical in function

3# God is not stuck on one style of anything—preaching praying and singing, etc.

4# It's about your <u>soul</u>, and not just comfort.

5# Absolutely, under no circumstances is the church ever for anybody's entertainment

<u>Becoming a Part</u>

Being a part of your local church is one of the greatest things you could do: by advancing the kingdom of God, by impacting your community with His Love, and His word being displayed in action. God uses His church like the United States uses its embassies in other countries. We are His ambassadors on earth and we all have different roles and responsibilities, so when you select a church you have to make sure you understand the mission of the church and the vision of the pastor immediately after becoming a member.

1 Corinthians 14:40
New King James Version (NKJV)

Let all things be done decently and <u>in order.</u>

Why is this important?
Understanding the mission of the church helps you understand where your gift fits in; understanding the vision of the pastor lets you know how to apply it. God has blessed everyone with gifts, but this does not give anybody the right to

come into any ministry as a freelancing member. Anybody can have the gifts; but the million dollar question is: *Is this gift usable and in order?* The exit door hinges of the church are on fire, unfortunately, because there are so many people with the gifts who will refuse to work in order, based on independent thought. Though this is not the church's largest problem, great opportunities for very gifted people are lost because they will not submit themselves under anybody's leadership. Submission allows you to get closer for deeper revelation and clearer understanding, while rejection keeps you stagnated and confused.

Submission is not domination, but it is strength under control that is managed and dispensed properly. There are many forces in nature where this principle is displayed. If they were not harnessed and regulated, our attempts to use them for the good would be very deadly. The same principle applies; the truth is, gifted people will tear up more than they accomplish because they refuse to submit under leadership. By doing this they neglect the opportunities that come along with obedience. Obedience is something that always opens the door for favor; when you are obedient, favor is looking for you. Many things unlock and unfold to you when you choose to connect yourself with the mission and vision that God has given to the ministry you're part of.

Whether you are newly a part of a ministry or have been a part of it for a long time, I urge and encourage you to pray that God places this ministry and vision of your pastor in your heart. This will allow you, in prayer and in spirit, to become one with the mission and vision that God has placed you under.

Matthew 18:19-20
New King James Version (NKJV)
"Again I say to you that if two of you agree on earth concerning anything that they ask, it will be done for them by My Father in heaven. For where two or three are gathered together in My name, I am there in the midst of them."

Satan is very clear on his agenda against the church, but I'm not exactly sure if the body of Christ fully understands his methods and ways. I think it's evident through time that Satan cannot destroy the church; if he could, it would've been destroyed a long time ago. However, I believe that there are three things that he masters.

Illusions

A mental condition characterized by delusions of persecution, unwarranted jealousy, or exaggerated self-importance, typically elaborated into an organized system.

He plays tricks on your mind by making you see things that are not there, getting you to notice things that are not even relevant or factual. He sparks paranoia by these illusions, and this will either leave you feeling condemned or ridiculed for no apparent reason.

Deception
The action of deceiving someone...

This normally happens when people have the intentions to do something good, but do it in a way that is not in the original design or order. Deception will also cause you to believe your way, over God's word. It can even lead you to the point where you would adamantly argue, debate, and even fight over something you know in your heart of hearts is wrong.

Ventriloquism

A person who can speak or utter sounds so that they seem to come from somewhere else, especially an entertainer who makes their voice appear to come from a dummy.

This is especially important to know and understand, since Satan is a master of illusions and the father of deceptions. He will use people who are accessible to him to come against you; just when you focus your energy in one area, he projects his voice to sing as if he's coming from another place.

Have you ever been in a disagreement with somebody, and you thought for sure you had all of the facts together; but, to your surprise, found that there were many things that you were unclear on? And after this disagreement, you still came up with no solution to the problem? Do you know why? Because the energy you devoted into them was misdirected—they were never the issue or the problem from the beginning. Satan has the ability to throw his voice; you can be working diligently in your church, then all of a sudden things will break out at home. And when you start devoting your time *at home* and not the ministry you have been assigned to, you'll find yourself in a never-ending situation. You'll ask yourself, *'how did I even get into this*?' Here's how: while you devote your attention to one urgent matter, you leave certain duties uncovered and certain responsibilities undone—so while you are away, Satan wreaks havoc. That's why in certain situations it's best to fight the enemy by staying focused on what you're doing.

These are the methods and the tools that he uses to disarm the connections in our lives. The mind is a battleground because of the open doorways we leave in our emotions and thought processes. Satan is well aware of the power of agreement; this is why he works overtime to make sure that when you get into the house of God you feel no sense of connection—and even apathy towards a relationship with God. This principle causes us to have what I would call a **miss connection**—this is something that happens when we get together, but we're not prepared to properly process a relationship. It also can happen when we're still holding onto an old mindset from previous connections to a person, place, or thing. But you're now in a completely different environment. You're in a completely different arena, and you have to move beyond what your mind keeps bringing you back into: old traditions and dogmatic practices. Any time you will not evolve in your mind, you rob yourself of greater opportunities for new relationships. There are certain miracles in life that will only happen once you begin to understand the importance of other people.

"A connection is a terrible thing to waste"

Don't waste time chasing down things that don't matter. What it takes you away from is the purpose that you even came to church, and that is to worship and serve God and to become a soul-winning witness for Him. Stay focused.

Special Entrances

Here's a story that I'm not necessarily proud of, but it is true. One night after a rehearsal, my bass player, Tommy, and I were riding home. All of a sudden, he says to me, "do you have a couple of minutes to spare? I need you to take me downtown."

"It's cool I'm not doing anything," I replied. Then he asked, "do you have your keyboard in the trunk?"

"Yeah I do," I answered.

"Okay, I just wanted to know", was his reply.

About 10 minutes later we were driving up to the Pyramid Arena, and as we were driving up I noticed a sign that said, "SPECIAL EVENT PARKING IN THE REAR". Tommy said that's where we were going, to the rear. Moments later we were getting out of the car and I said to him, "are you going to see somebody?"

"Something like that", he answered. "Open your trunk so I can get my guitar, and—by the way—grab your keyboard."

"Wait a minute Tommy, what are we doing?"

He said, "Man, I got you—just follow me and let me do all the talking."

At this point I'm thinking, *he plays guitar for a lot of different groups.* He was walking really fast up to the security guard and he mentioned something to them; as I got closer I heard him say, "the musicians on stage are sick and we are the replacements, we need to go in right now!" The security guard paused for about 3 seconds and got on his radio. He asked for ID; he looked at Tommy's and let him in, then he took my ID. Tommy said, "this is Al Green's nephew, and one of his musicians", so the security guard began to ask me questions about some of the people at the church, and I answered the questions correctly. At this time, another security guard came up; they took our bags and escorted us through the back entrance. As we moved briskly through the hallway going to the rear of the main stage, I noticed a voice on stage that sounded very familiar to me; trying to keep my poker face together, I said to myself, *is that Ronald Isley on stage?* About that time, I saw him standing in all-white, singing "I want to groove with you", as Tommy and I went through the special entrance. We both thanked the security guards, and as they walked off I hit Tommy on the arm and said, "why didn't you tell me we were coming here?"

"Because I knew you wouldn't have wanted to go if I told you," he said, "and I would have just missed out on this opportunity; man, this is good music."

I stood there in amazement, for two reasons: number one, I couldn't believe he got me in there, and number two, I couldn't believe how good they sounded in person.

Have you ever wondered why people can't get rid of some attitudes they have? Or why it's difficult for you to shake anger and rage on the inside? A lot of times, when these things take over we are really not ourselves; to some degree, it's as though we are prisoners of our own emotions. The minute you try to have a good day, something always brings you back into that emotional jail cell; and even though you may blame others and others may have wronged you, deep within yourself you have no idea where all the rage and anger is coming from. Even though you won't admit it to other people, you know some small situations are taken way out of proportion; and even when others try to seek a resolution with you, anger and aggression leave a residue in your attitude. In the next phase of this process, you become despondent and distant as you begin to feel that nobody understands who you are and what you're going through. Though you talk to people, you still feel as though nobody sees or hears you. The third phase is when you begin to seek attention. This attention comes from people that you hope will see what you're going through and the agony that you are facing by the expression on your face. Unfortunately, this is *not* a tactic that works all the time because one of two things may happen: you either get attention from someone you *don't* want to get attention from; or the person you were hoping would finally notice says nothing to you. The fourth phase that kicks in is despair; you feel all alone, and through your emotions you ask, *how did this happen?*

I believe one of the greatest doors that Satan uses to get into our minds is the doorway of our emotions. When he gains access to your emotions he can fly under your radar undetected, and push certain buttons for you to fall into a place of apathy. Some say Satan is absolutely marvelous with a paintbrush; instead of a masterpiece he will give you a "disaster piece". We know that Satan is a deceiver and a manipulator. Well, rarely do you hear people say how he gets in. Let me tell you, he uses the doorway of your emotions—it's a perfect way to get right into your mind. Here's the process:

He always tries to come through another way
He always uses lie to getting in
He always uses things that you're familiar with, as a form of enticement, to get through the door
He always brings baggage in—weight for you to carry
He always gives too much, so we can corrupt ourselves with excess
He wants to leave you really conflicted and confused

It is his plan and goal to keep the door of your emotions wide open for inadequacy, low self-esteem, and low self-worth to come in behind him. All of these things desire to set up shop in the recesses of your mind.

Matthew 12:43-45
New Living Translation (NLT)
"When an evil spirit leaves a person, it goes into the desert, seeking rest but finding none. Then it says, 'I will return to the person I came from.' So it returns and finds its former home empty, swept, and in order. Then the spirit finds seven other spirits more evil than itself, and they all enter the person and live there. And so that person is worse off than before. That will be the experience of this evil generation."

Jesus is speaking in this particular text to give us an opportunity to look at things from a spiritual viewpoint, which only He can give us. Jesus gives us vital points that we should definitely pay attention to if we're going to live the life that He has called us to live, and not revert back into the things of the past.

I think one of the vital points that Jesus makes in this text is, when spirits are released they desire to come back. The next thing to pay attention to is that spirits look for places to rest; so this is an indication to us that spirits need a place to reside.

When it returns, it finds that the person has swept the house and put things in order. And this is exactly right; instead of fortifying our house, we would rather beautify it with things that make us feel comfortable. Because we have gone through certain circumstances in life, we feel that we are taking a little "Me Time" to straighten up our lives and put things right back the way they used to be. It's just like grandmother's house:

even though the front door was locked, if I wanted to get in, all I'd have to do was go around to the side entrance because, for some reason or another, she always left that door open. This is exactly how Satan uses our emotions: as an entrance to get right back in—but he does not come alone.

Here's a scenario of how these spirits work: you may have struggled with fornication (sex before marriage) and when you cast it out and it leaves, you feel as you have everything under control. You put yourself back together and try to go back to some sense of normalcy to keep your mind from it; but you hold on to bitterness from previous situations. This becomes an entrance to allow fornication right back in, along with jealousy, pride, and other demons that will lay dormant until the right time. These demons will manipulate situations to work out so that they use *you* to fulfill *their* passion. If it is pride, Satan will bless you with a lot of material things so you can be prideful; if it's the lust for sex, he will always place you around people who are your type, so that you can fulfill that passion. This is the reason why he needs an entrance to your body. He's committed to twisting your emotions and feelings in whatever direction he needs to keep the entrance open.

The next thing I want you to notice from the scripture is that the house was empty—this is a critical point. Ephesians 5:18 says, "be filled with the Holy Spirit." It's not enough to just get things *out* of your life, but what are you *filling* your life with? You have to feed your faith in order to safeguard your own emotions with the word of God. The only way that dormant demons will leave your mind is when you take the necessary steps to make the word of God a necessity in your everyday life. Don't just pick up a Bible alone, but also invest your money into commentaries that will help you break the Scriptures down for you so that they are understandable, and so that you can apply them. Once you apply them, then you can do as the Scripture said in:

2 Corinthians 10:5
King James Version (KJV)
Casting down imaginations, and every high thing that exalteth itself against the knowledge of God, and bringing into captivity every thought to the obedience of Christ;

Be filled with the Spirit of God, and close off the entrance.

Sheepskin coats

This is a very popular statement that has been used to cast a negative light on the men and women of God that do God's work. Now, I must admit there have been some major blows to the body of Christ and to the image of preachers; however, I call sin a sin and error an error—but there's always grace, no matter who has done wrong. I do not think that this is the proper prescription for these particular people, and I also think that if we only prescribe it to clergy, we've missed the true essence of what is being stated, so let's break it down.

This phrase derives from an iconic sermon from Jesus, which is known as the Sermon on the Mount, located in Matthews chapter 7. Take a closer look at the text; I believe that it is saying something profound and prolific. The letters are written in red, meaning Jesus spoke them. Verse 15 of this chapter starts off by saying beware of false prophets, so the text is immediately addressing gifted people who come to you in sheep's clothing; who dress themselves up in humility to blend in with the rest of the sheep. The next part of the text states that inwardly they are ravenous wolves. Here, Jesus reveals the eye of the shepherd: the ability to spot the difference between his sheep. We can be swayed by a person's gift, to the extent that we overlook their character and allow them to do things based on their ability to flow in service.

How many of us pastors have sacrificed standards, values, and things that we have worked years to establish—just because a person had a gift and we saw advancement in our ministry? How many church leaders have allowed themselves to be manipulated by gifted wolves that had a personal agenda? The fact that the wolf is in sheep's clothing is a clear sign of deception; this is the inward workings of Satan. He works through trickery and deception, and through this illustration that Jesus gives us, we see that Satan wants to penetrate the body of Christ in order to destroy. Unfortunately, some yield to his plan—and that gives them free access into the body of Christ; but I encourage you to have the heart, and mind, and most of all, the *eye* of your shepherd/ pastor/leader. You are probably saying, *"how can I safeguard myself and my ministry from wolves?"* Jesus gives us a bona fide way to safeguard ourselves from this type of attack on our ministries in the next verse:

Matthew 7: 16-18
New King James Version (NKJV)
You will know them by their fruits. Do men gather grapes from thornbushes or figs from thistles? Even so, every good tree bears good fruit, but a bad tree bears bad fruit. A good tree cannot bear bad fruit, nor can a bad tree bear good fruit.

He gives us cut-and-dried principles to counteract this type of attack by using foresight. We cannot be enamored by a person's gift, but persuaded only by fruit. You cannot fall for persuasive conversation and sympathy tricks in church; pay attention to the *fruit*, and I even dare say, don't look at their faithfulness, look at their fruit—the reason being, everybody is faithful. The question is, *what are you faithful to*? There are certain people who are only faithful because of the social connection they get from the people at church. They really don't have the heart or mind of the leader, nor are they concerned about the mission or vision of the church. Sometimes people come for networking, or to pick up new lovers. Whatever the case may be, keep your eyes on the fruit.

Sweep under the pews

I must confess that sometimes life is rough, and being a pastor doesn't make it easier. But I have found tranquility in the church; this one simple thing is a very enlightening and personal time with God. When I arrive at the church early in the morning, before anyone is there or I start my morning schedule, I love to sweep under the pews and talk to God. During this time, I have intimate talks with God and express myself, and I can hear His voice so clearly. The other side of this process of sweeping is that sometimes you can find some <u>unbelievable</u> stuff under the pews. Sometimes there can be all types of trash under the pews; at other times there are even valuable things under the pews.

So I ask you, what are you going to do when the worship service is over? When the singing, shouting, and dancing is over and the thought-provoking sermon is done; what are you going to do when you are really trying to get close to God and apply the word to your own life—and you find something under your neighbors pew? The fact of the matter is, *every* person has some issue they're trying to deal with. There are different levels of faith that everybody is on, and unfortunately your expectation is not always met regarding where *you* think they should be. That would be extremely judgmental and self-righteous to come into any environment and say what people should be doing. You have to grow to the understanding that, whenever you're trying to get close to God, Satan tries to leave you feeling as though you have unearthed truths about other people that cause you to cast judgment by saying *"Nobody's living right in the church"*. The more you buy into this, the more you lose faith yourself. I believe that if you follow a person long enough, you will find something; you will find an issue, a fault, or some character defect that you may use to disqualify them. I suggest to you that doing this is not wise. The more that you do this, the more you take the attention away from connecting with God. That was the whole purpose of joining anyway, right?

So if you found somebody else's trash, it would be better for you to just keep sweeping and talking to God; I understand clearly that there have been many times when somebody else has to sweep up my mess.

God has not called us to condemn, but He has called us to love and serve each other in the spirit of meekness; we must have this mindset if we are going to be the church that Jesus wants to see upon His return. Don't allow information about your neighbor [that is volunteered from other people] to throw you into a tailspin about the church. You have to understand; when people are making a desperate effort to volunteer information to you, ask yourself a very critical question: *why do I need to know this?* The second question to ask yourself after that is, *how does this information pertain to or support the reason that I joined?*

Do things to be seen at church

I know we have always been taught traditionally that you shouldn't do things just to be seen in church; even though I understand this, let's examine a few things.

Let's look at this from another standpoint: what would happen if we saw more men and women being active in churches across America? Do you know the phenomenal impact that would have on our communities, our jail systems, our sons and daughters, our families? It would dramatically change our way of life if one simple thing was displayed, and that is divine order. Can you imagine the impact this would have on the negative forces behind our cultures and those that push satanic agendas through media?

It would be phenomenal. We would be able to shift our culture if we would stand up for what we believe; we have to stand out. The fact of the matter is, we have to change our culture by setting a different example—not just on the outside, but from the inside. We're living in a culture where people not only want to see the *display* but also the inner workings; we can tell people all day long how to do something but if we don't demonstrate what we're saying, it is a lost cause. So in order for people to take us seriously we have to show sincere humility, mercy, love, and forgiveness. All of these things and much more make our faith relevant and tangible; now it is our task to get it out.

It's not really difficult. Even if you are a person who is not outgoing but tends to be more laid-back, your personal testimony may be exactly the tool that God will use to bring souls to Christ. Have you ever wondered why you went through something specifically that others haven't? It is possible that God allowed you to go through those things so that your testimony could be an undeniable experience with Him that causes other believers to be strengthened, and the unsaved to be reconciled to Him. By the troubles, struggles, and circumstances that you have been through, He is ordained for this very purpose: that He might win souls.

Have you ever watched a movie and during the movie you identify who is the villain and the hero; then suddenly there's a twist in the story and the villain has now joined the side of the hero? That's exactly how God wants to use you—as the 'inside man' the person on the inside who's going to make the story change for the good because you stood up and stood out. I will go as far as saying that if you want your family to change, it has to begin with you. Let everybody see the change that has happened in your life. If you have been saved a long time, and tried witnessing to your family but it seems as though it has not worked, don't be weary in well-doing. Keep going, keep standing up and being the light. Even if you have failed and your family has personally seen you fall, that is not a reason for you to be ashamed; stand up—show everybody God's mercy and forgiveness for you, and that He has mercy and forgiveness for them. We are living in a day and time where we have to speak out and stand up if we're going to be the church of Jesus Christ.

Silence is deadly. That's why I encourage you to be the voice that God is using to speak to the world; be the hands that He uses to touch your community.

Chapter 10

Are you led to lead?

Moving to the front of the church

I believe that, to understand this particular principle about leadership, we have to understand the goal of the church. Without question, we are doing all we do to win souls for Christ. One of the key purposes of the church is to energize, motivate, and inspire non-believers and convert them into true believers, winning souls for Christ. In order to do this, we need to have great leadership to bring us to a place of success.

No, everyone cannot go their own way, or be led by their feelings. As a body, we must think with one mind. To arrive at a particular goal we have to all plan strategically; we must go in that direction *on purpose*, not by chance or accident. Success is something that never happens by chance or randomness, but it is achieved by working hard with a goal in mind. It is more than having a reserve seat in church, standing up front, or demanding respect from people. You can't be "goal-driven", you have to be driven by your *purpose* and *passion* to complete the job successfully. Goals are set when you only allow yourself to work to a certain point; when you work in your purpose, you are committed to the end.

If you want to be a leader there are a few things we need to go over. We can't fall into the mindset that every outcome of our leadership is the will of God. Here's why: if I am given a test and I don't study for it—and I fail the test because I did not know the information—can I just say that was the will of God? Of course not! It is required of me to study, so when it comes down to doing something for God, I have to be accountable. Without this understanding of accountability I can easily hide all of my laziness and rebellion under the umbrella of *"maybe that was not the will of God for me to do it"*. Keep in mind that God is sovereign; He is the king over all His creations. We don't have a hand in His purpose. God has entrusted us with dominion, and with that dominion comes *responsibility* and *accountability.*

Energetic enthusiasm will last for a moment, but the trust that you need from people as a leader is built with consistency and can last a lifetime. Both integrity and character have to be consistently developed in the life of a leader. When leaders have no integrity, it pulls the curtains back on their enthusiasm and makes their efforts look like a show.

Great communication is also an invaluable tool for success in leadership. This concept is made up of three components:

1# Communicating with the general purpose

Colossians 4:6
New Living Translation (NLT)

Let your conversation be gracious and attractive so that you will have the right response for everyone.

Understanding this particular principle allows you to effectively communicate with the people you are leading. You can have excellent ideas, but if you have not effectively learned how to communicate them, it can be beyond frustrating. You'll end up watching opportunities pass you by because you have not mastered a delivery that connects you with your audience. It may not always be other people rejecting you, however reluctantly; there comes a point when you have to examine your delivery, take your personal feelings out of what you want to say, and get down to the 'brass tacks'. Make each one of your points clear and effective, then you can move forward. If you communicate effectively, you won't have to move alone.

#2 Motivated to move

Numbers 13:30-32
New Living Translation (NLT)
But Caleb tried to quiet the people as they stood before Moses. "Let's go at once to take the land," he said. "We can certainly conquer it!" But the other men who had explored the land with him disagreed. "We can't go up against them! They are stronger than we are!" So they spread this bad report about the land among the Israelites: "The land we traveled through and explored will devour anyone who goes to live there. All the people we saw were huge.

Don't get stuck! There comes a time in leadership when your position is no longer new, when the enthusiasm and celebrations are over and 'the rubber meets the road', so to speak. At this point, you have to perform. Often, what stifles leaders is the amount of outside views and opinions from others; this can be depleting. However, when you walk in leadership you are called to go higher, and push harder. You cannot allow yourself to be stuck in the mud of other people's thoughts and opinions. Your responsibility is to take direction from your leader, apply it, and bring back the most positive report. Be the Joshua and Caleb of your leadership; let your purpose connect with your passion and go for it! Be allergic to comfort, and tackle all adversity because victory is on the other side of it. You will never make it if you're not motivated to move. You have to be absolutely content when it comes to understanding that everyone who is part of your leadership team may not share the same motivation and joy that you do. Still, keep moving! Don't allow others' perception of the giant obstacles get in the way, or quiet the voice of your God-given instincts. Don't allow others' lack of enthusiasm and momentum to make you docile; be the change that is needed and that you're looking for.

3# Following Orders

Everybody cannot do his or her own thing spiritually. I don't care how anointed you are, there is still protocol and order that God would never negate. **This is a modern-day heresy that you don't need affirmation from your leader!**

Contrary to popular belief, the spirit can flow in order. Notice in 1Corinthians chapter 14 it talks about speaking in tongues, prophecy, and ordering church, but it ends by saying

in verse 40, *"Let all things be done decently and in order."*

Ironically, it's amazing how difficult it is for some people to follow protocol; if you're going to operate under leadership, you have to understand that you *yourself* have to be led. In a church setting, leaders—whether they are a part of an auxiliary or ministry—are a fixture of what the ministry is all about, which sets the climate of the church. You have to remember that leadership is *influence*, not just position; though position is a part of it, leadership has more to do with influence.

When you are a leader, you cannot have a small revolt surrounding you. This is a sign that there is a secret rebellion going on within you. Instead of influencing people, you have now infected them with your personal dislikes and your hidden agendas against other people. When the members in your revolt carry out your orders by their actions, deeds, and plans, you are still infecting the vision.

You are the provision to the vision; any time a church has two visions, it become stagnated and dwindles because of confusion—and this is exactly what Satan wants.

I encourage you to submit your gift under your leader. In due time, you will be exalted if you are patient. If God sent you there, don't become impatient. There is danger ahead when you work in a gift and you have not been properly released and properly covered by someone that God has put in your life. **(Acts 19:13-16)**

Open Vents

Being a leader in the church does not exempt you from challenging times. Not at all; in many cases, being a leader in the church causes you to balance your purpose with your problems. Due to stressful situations, leaders often don't have opportunities to take long vacations. I have found that most of us work through those things and often find some solitude in the work of the ministry. The problem lies in that, even though we are doing the work of the ministry, we still haven't found a safe place to unload. Sadly, for some leaders this solitude is something we can't find even in our residence. If you have nowhere for these frustrating issues to release, the pressure within yourself begins to mount—and you'll find yourself leading while internally bleeding. Statistically, there are large numbers of people who are carrying ministries on their backs while on the verge of giving up. With all of these issues to balance between ministry and your personal life, it can throw your mind into a cyclone. In an effort to hold everything together, you put on a smile and serve on 'auto pilot'. You know things have gotten really bad for you personally when you can see the effects of your gift working in a positive way—people are being inspired and uplifted—yet in that moment you are frustrated, because nobody sees that you are on the verge of breaking. Everything that you are carrying internally is causing you to crumble. Others are completely oblivious to your problems because of the mask that you wear during service times; so out of desperation, you find someone to vent to. The person seems completely harmless and convenient at the time, but don't get too comfortable.

Here's a principle that I learned while resolving some maintenance issue at the church.

Your ventilation system has to meet regulation requirements, or it can create more issues. This is a principle we need to transfer into leadership. When you are venting to somebody, you have to make sure that they are strong enough and regulated enough in their own character. Keep in mind, the "venting process" can go horribly wrong, because once you've snapped out of it and feel better, you have now leaked out exhaust fumes. That release now contaminates the atmosphere in which you serve. When you're back on board and try again to rally your troops, you find reluctance and resistance, and your leadership ability is not as effective. What happened? By venting, you have infected them with your personal feelings towards certain decisions and directions of the church. This is especially detrimental when you try to advocate publicly for something you are against privately; this leaves your new comrades scratching their heads, because they shared your position against the things that you felt were wrong. Now, you run the risk of them exposing everything you've said to them in private; they may view you as a traitor, or in church terms, a "hypocrite".

Leaders can't do this!

When you need someone to talk to first:

- Make special time and effort in prayer and reading the word of God to find solutions and answers to your questions or problems.
- Go to the person that is over you, with a listening ear ready to receive understanding.
- Do not ask the opinions of other people or congregants

A third of the angels

You have influence; whether you know it or not and contrary to your belief, your voice has power. Your voice absolutely has authority. When you are a believer, you have to know and understand that it's almost as though you live your life with the cameras always rolling—and what you say *can* be used for or <u>against</u> you. This goes especially for people who are in leadership. What you say is very important, and absolutely needs to be governed by the Holy Spirit because you can contaminate your own atmosphere. The worst thing you can do is willingly and purposefully tear down the house of God. Regardless of how you may feel that you have been wronged, the best possible solution is to completely leave the situation alone, rather than take action and influence people with negativity. By doing this willingly, you become an adversary against God's plan and an advantage to Satan.

I think it's vitally important that we understand that our emotions can be a doorway for a satanic encroachment against God's purpose and plan for our lives. So before you "blackout", and begin to open your mouth without a bridle, be careful—you don't want to put yourself against God, even though you have been hurt. I agree that being hurt by people in the church is very difficult to process, and can be crippling to your faith. To get over the hurt can be a challenge of its own, because a lot of us come into churches already broken, torn down, hurt, and confused. We don't expect to be hurt in a safe place, which I totally understand. What is key to know and fully understand is that He has not called us to use our emotions as a valid reason to violate His word, whether we're hurt or not. He has still given us direct commands on how to treat each other.

Church was never intended to be the wild, wild West; you can't assemble a posse and go your own way with your own rules. Bringing people to church is one thing, but *driving* them away is something you should be very scared of. Just because you have a disagreement with someone it does not give you the right to 'take back' the people you brought into the church; and if they follow you, what position do you hold over them, that you have now become their sub-leader or pew pastor? When this happens, people are playing on loyalty and you force them to be committed to your cause. In an effort to ease the conflict, they may choose to opt out altogether rather than endure your sympathy tricks, or sit in the pew and feel badly. Most if not all disagreements, dislikes, splits, and fallouts are due to the lack of one simple principle that Jesus gave us:

"Love your neighbor as yourself". If we would just apply this principle to our entire lives and not just church, the world would be ten times better. Love is so important, He did not leave it up to us to define it, and he gave us His definition:

1 Corinthians 13:4-7
New Living Translation (NLT)
Love is patient and kind. Love is not jealous or boastful or proud or rude. It does not demand its own way. It is not irritable, and it keeps no record of being wronged.
It does not rejoice about injustice but rejoices whenever the truth wins out. Love never gives up, never loses faith, is always hopeful, and endures through every circumstance.

What kind of leader are you?

Leadership is a VERB ...not a NOUN

What is a Verb Leader?

VERB-Leaders are people <u>Updated for Action</u> and ready to fulfill vision by executing tasks and building relationships.

The mindset of a verb leader asks *"how do I connect them to what I'm passionate about?"*

They are getting things done and influencing others to do the same.

They can be placed in other positions that are not their **<u>Calling,</u>** without being offended or disgruntled, and can still be a **strong** support. They will always listen for planning and direction, because they don't want to spend unnecessary energy on secret strategies that don't come from the leader.

They have to learn how to turn **frustration into fuel.**

It's important that we gravitate to the type of leadership that is consistently moving forward and proactive and interactive with all people at all times.

Ephesians 5:15-18
New Living Translation (NLT)

So be careful how you live. Don't live like fools, but like those who are wise. Make the most of every opportunity in these evil days. Don't act thoughtlessly, but understand what the Lord wants you to do. Don't be drunk with wine, because that will ruin your life. Instead, be filled with the Holy Spirit,

Colossians 4:5-6
New Living Translation (NLT)

Live wisely among those who are not believers, and make the most of every opportunity.

Let your conversation be gracious and attractive so that you will have the right response for everyone.

John 9:4
New Living Translation (NLT)
We *must quickly carry out the tasks assigned us by the one who sent us. The night is coming, and then no one can work.*

There is no magic moment in leadership, you have to make it happen. It is the productive mentality that causes success. Leadership should be defined when you are putting out 100% of yourself. Therefore, you have no time to waste in anything that is unproductive, because you are called to action.

A Noun Leader, on the other hand, is concerned with different aspects of being a leader. Their focus and drive is on who's doing it; where they're doing it; and what they're doing or using to get it done.

They spend more time and investigation on who has the position. According to their feelings, they will either disqualify the person or they will support them. They will methodically look for errors to discredit and undo the work that another person hasn't done, simply because they don't like them.

A Noun Leader will covet and can be territorial over their position. Even if the job is not being done, they still want to be the only person in charge over it, or to make sure they hinder whoever they do not want working on the task.

They always take feedback and interpret it as an attack from the enemy. They can't be persuaded to do anything else, because they don't want to be moved.

They will never listen to the people's lead, because their position is about self-gratification and not group edification.

Place

Their mindset is, *"I'm only a leader at church"*. They never take the opportunity to influence or to be a light in any other environment.

They are not interested in church development, because if the charge is to develop and grow, it will create more responsibility and require more of them. That's why you'll find these individuals expressing subtle rebellions against the vision of an organization, because progress threatens the familiarity of the place.

Noun Leaders only transform into leaders when they are in a particular environment or "place". The minute they step out of the door, the characteristics and disciplines of a leader are not evident. They often associate their leadership position with that environment or "place" and once they are not in that place anymore, they're not in leadership. In return, their accountability and actions are out the window. They're on their own, and they do whatever they want to do because they're not at the place; but the liability here is that there will be people who see you *outside* and *inside* of the place, and most people may process this lapse of integrity as hypocritical.

Thing

This aspect really kicks in when a person has been in a position for a long period of time, and either has to share the position or is required to be accountable to other people in higher positions. They become possessive and bossy when it comes to them being in charge of any task. The minute they are not in charge, they seem uncooperative because they feel that they should be doing the task alone; it's theirs, and help is viewed as an intrusion.

They will only be committed and driven on their own project, and don't look at anything that doesn't pertain to their task directly. They'll make self-centered decisions and complaints that are centered around a small group of people instead of serving everybody.

The next thing you'll see in the project that they are in charge of is a lot of exclusion; they'll refuse to work with other people because they fear other ideas. They will never accept that something is not wrong just because it's not done the same way they would do it. They will make statements such as:

"After my thing is over I'm leaving, I have something else to do I'm only coming because I'm doing my thing".

"If you don't like it, I can do my thing at another church".

This type of mindset will be detrimental to the growth and development of the new church.

You have to change your thinking in order to receive direction from God. Just as there are multiple parts under the hood of a car that work simultaneously to make the vehicle drivable; the failure of some parts can damage other parts and possibly cause the car to stop running altogether. If the motor goes out in your car but you just installed a new battery, you're going to have problems still. You have to fix the core of the problem, and you will be running in pristine condition.

Green Note

Throughout this journey we have touched on various situations, circumstances, and different areas of life. My prayer is that you have seen the common thread that runs through them all. What is key to remember is that you can't go through life without being connected to somebody; contrary to popular belief, you need people. A wise person said, *"if you can do everything yourself, then you're not working towards your destiny, and your dream is not big enough"*. My prayer is that this book helps you make some of the greatest decisions in your life. There are some decisions that you're going to make now that directly affect the relationships in any arena that you are in. I also pray that the connections that you're going to make based on future decisions will allow you to go into the world with a new mind, ready to give 110%. Be prepared to receive everything the new connection in your life has for you. By applying these principles, you will be ready to walk in your "God-given" authority. I encourage you to be the best 'you' ever! I believe that the seasons of missed opportunities are over! This is the right place, this is the right time and, more importantly, this is the right you. Now you are armed and dangerous, loaded with new information that will phenomenally change every situation that you have been afforded.

You're ready to meet the love of your life, and will not be weighed down by past decisions and mistakes you once made. Now you can tear down the walls of exclusion because you know what to expect on the other side, plus, this time you're stronger. Now, you can balance your time, manage your priorities, and give your relationships the oxygen that they need. Now, you can clean your closet of the things from the past, and make room for the things you will need to sustain the relationships in your life.

I speak good health and blessings over you, because the stressful relationships are gone, and you have connected yourself to the right ones. Your life is full of adventure and fulfillment because you have changed your mind. Your work relationships are now productive for you; you have now become an asset to your superiors. You will no longer allow dormant demons to extract life out of you. You are free from bad connections!

That This Book will Connect The Right You To The Right People....

About the Author

Pastor Robert L. Green

Robert L. Green currently serves at Redemption Ministries, located in the Cedar Rapids and North Liberty Iowa as Senior Pastor.

In 1991 he began his journey in the music ministry at the age of 14. He sharpened his musical skills while he served in his family's ministry: Full Gospel Tabernacle under the leadership of Rev. Al Green. At the age of 21, Robert L. Green accepted his divine purpose and received his ministerial license in 2001. A Preacher of the Gospel, he relentlessly teaches and serves his congregation from the practical principles in the word of God. Pastor Green has traveled abroad preaching and teaching the word of God, inspiring and encouraging through music. His influence goes beyond the "four walls of church" and extends to the community of our city and beyond.

Other books from the Author
I Decided to be Blessed
Silly Women and Sleepy Men

Twitter

https://twitter.com/RobertLGreen11

Facebook

https://www.facebook.com/RobertGreenOnline

Google +

https://plus.google.com/+Robertgreenonline

E-Mail

Joinedthebook@gmail.com

Coming in Fall 2014

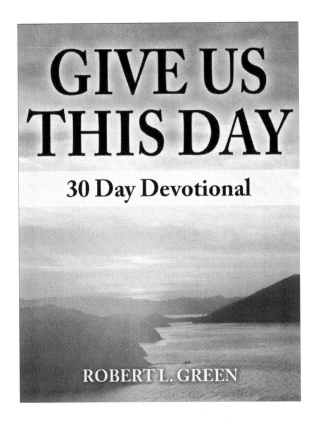

eBook (Only)

Made in the USA
Charleston, SC
14 November 2014